Beyond Cuddle Party

How Pajamas, Human Connection and
11 Rules Can Change Your Life

Monique Darling

Juicy Enlightenment
Orem, UT

Edited by Lisa Fornier, Doug and Tina Gross, Leonard Rosenbaum
Cover Design/Art Direction : Rob Actis-Actis Creative
Cover Design : Christian Fuenfhausen
Interior Design/Art Direction: Rob Actis-Actis Creative
Interior Formatting: Chris Derrick
Cuddle Cover Photo : Rob Actis-Actis Creative
Author Photo : Theresa Vargo
Rear Cover Image (Tricycle) : Avid Awake

Cover Photo Cuddlers -Tanya Dehler, Susanne Woodward, Amy Otto,
Stephanie Pearlman, Ken Blair, Vladimir Martyanov, Wayne Kavil,
Laura Hightower, Carrie Smith-Hardee, Abram Pena, Michelle Harrison

ISBN 978-0-9906268-0-0

Contents

Acknowledgements

There are so many people that made this journey, this book possible!

I will name a few, but I also want to thank the many, each of you who has ever read one of my vulnerable Facebook posts, has ever attended a Cuddle Party, has told a loved one they should really attend a Cuddle Party, especially each of you who has ever taken the time to write, call, text, or in some way express to me what cuddle party and its rules has meant your life. Thank you!

My first thank you is to ME! A great big thank you for the courage to continuously take this path, to fully experiment and live as uniquely me.

Thank you Nathan Darling, my dear brave, spectacular sons, my Mom and siblings, (especially you grandma, supporting me from the other side) thank you for being there with me for this entire journey, for holding my tears, encouraging me through my greatest fears, loving me even as I changed all the usual rules of engagement of how a family relates.

Thank you Peter Petersen, for coming on such an extended magical mystery tour, in the spacious freedom and unconditional love you offer in every breath, I am constantly brought into a deeper remembrance of who I am, and permission to explore and be even more than that. Thank you for letting your soul shine so brightly!

Thank you Reid Mihalko for creating Cuddle Party, for taking it to the world, for finding me, seeing me, encouraging me, helping me find my voice.

Thank you Shawn Roop for never letting me over give, for the space to know I never needed to impress you, I never ever need to do anything for/with you. Because, me, exactly as I am, is the gift.

Thank you Lawrence Lanoff for the gift of ever expanding what's possible, showing me within my body, experiential reference points of how infinite possibilities feel. And for the gift of no matter what I have ever thrown at you, your beautiful response has always been, "is that all you got, Monique?"

Thank you Kai Karrel for embodying magic, for meeting me in the creative field, for being the one who truly helped me find the way to fall in love with myself. Thank you for being my best friend.

Thank you Alex S. Morgan, for all the nights you held me as I struggled through a concept or idea, or all the times I thought this book was never going to be finished, was never going to be enough, your quiet love and support has meant everything to me!

Thank you Seva Khalsa for all the space you hold for every emotion to be felt and expressed fully, for your kind heart and peaceful spirit.

Thank you Charlie Glickman, for your command of words, for all the ways you constantly inspire me, especially in the joy and importance of truly learning to breath, let go, and be a great receiver.

Thank you David Cates for being the voice of unconditional acceptance, you are the very essence of nature, blowing through me, supporting my roots, helping me roll with the flow, and allowing the deepest fires and intensities to just burn through me, appreciating the refinement on the other side.

Thank you Destin Gerek for being one of the most vulnerable beings I have ever met. You are constantly inspiring me to get even more "naked" and I'm so grateful for your presence in my life.

Thank you Arden Leigh, for your gift with words, and for letting me see your ooey-gooey beautiful soft insides, thank you for owning your beauty, inside and out, for allowing me so deeply into your heart.

Thank you Eugene Hedlund for always meeting me as an equal, for helping me research and develop many of the ideas in this book and most of all for our shared philosophy of the beauty of "zero fucks given" as it leaves everyone free to choose how to be in every moment.

Thank you Kamala Devi for all the lessons and gifts you have given me on this long journey, for your example of being a bright star, for being the first "author" I really knew.

Thank you Scott Catamas for being my intro into compassionate communication, for being one of the very first people to offer to collaborate with me, for your generous spirit.

Thank you Matt Kahn for being one of my very first spiritual teachers/friends. Your message continues to resonate with me most of all "whatever is arising, love THAT"

Thank you Lisa Fornier, Leonard Rosenbaum, Doug and Tina Gross, for editing my baby with such skill and care, and one of the largest thank you's to (Lissa Woodson/Neighlani Kia) for giving me the game plan, for inspiring me to write, for being a great cheerleader and a huge support.

Thank you Rob Actis for your creative consulting, for your unwavering support, for taking this rough unpolished gemstone and adding your own professional flair to turn it into the masterpiece that it deserves to be.

Thank you Katie Weatherup, Pamela Madsen, Caroline Carrington, Kristina Millikan for being my sisters, my friends, my confidants, the people who dare to be ultra real with me and invite all of me to come play with you!

Thank you Jeanette Johnson, Rovena Sky, Gayle Roberts, Mitchell Jones, Hunter Gatherer Riley, Pu'uanuaha, Garden of Eden, Larry Michel, Valerie Gill, Julianne Parkinson, Leela Sullivan, Gina Anderson, Laurie Handlers, Meg Hunter, Bruce Bartlett, Tricia Sabo, Viktoria K, Robin Renee, Zahava Griss, Aurora Rae, Amanda Anatra, Darlene Jackson, Lucia Gabriela, Cathleene Cienfuegos, John LaughingHawk, Dana Sheridan, Dan Powers, Elizabeth Wood, Lakshmi Devi Luster, Darryl Duane, Ann Glucroft, Dr, Rusty Stewart, Brynn Bishop, Kelle Sparta, Sarah Taub, Michael Rios, Adam Paulman, and so many other amazing people for hosting and welcoming me and my events in your homes.

Thank you Marcia Baczynski, Betty Martin, Len Dailey, Reid Mihalko, Leela Sullivan, Edie Weinstein, Madelon Guinazzo and all the beautiful cuddle party facilitators I've gotten to interact with over the years. There are so many beautiful beings in my life, I honor each of you named and un-named in this acknowledgement page. Thank you for being YOU.

And my biggest thank you to God for being my best friend and constant cheerleader.

This book is for each of you

Foreword by Reid Mihalko

If you're a "maybe," say "no."

That's Cuddle Party Rule #5, and it's always been Cuddle Party Rule #5. When Monique Darling asked me to pen the foreword to *Cuddle Party: How Pajamas, Human Connection and 11 Rules Can Change Your Life*, her deadline was far enough in the distance that I said, "hell yes!" (as Monique would say) even though I was reluctant – which, in turn, means I was actually a "maybe," which means I should have said, "no."

How do I know I should have said no? Rule #5 (my favorite Cuddle Party rule, by the way) told me so. I blame Monique Darling for not taking my own advice. But it would take nearly a decade before we got to that part.

The Birth of Cuddle Party

The first Cuddle Party happened on an unseasonably mild day, February 29, 2004, approximately two weeks after I had the light-bulb idea that there was a way to teach non-massage therapists how to exchange safe, non-sexual touch, a.k.a. cuddling. And that first Cuddle Party almost never happhened.

Several decades ago, I was a martial artist who specialized in street combat, the opposite of cuddling. I had two black belts and a lot more muscle on my frame than I do today, and I was very good at taking people apart. Because I had the blessing of having several sensei (teachers) who taught me how to be a great teacher, and who encouraged my curiosity and "geekery," I eventually started studying how to put people back together. This led me to geeking out about massage, holistic healing, and energy-related healing techniques. I accumulated friendships with a dozen or so massage therapists and ardently traded massages with them to "steal" their massage "kung fu." This happened during my time as an actor and … wait for it … a bartender in New York City.

I was lucky enough to have my acting career take off, which impacted my availability to trade massages, which led to grumbling from my massage-trade buddies. Trust me, there's nothing more sad than a grumpy massage therapist, so I used my teaching geekery to concoct a monthly gathering where we could trade group, round-robin, multiple-handed massages. A brilliant solution, where everyone won! I could accomplish a month's worth of massage trades in a single night, introduce and (covertly) foist my trade buddies onto one another, and still get a great massage (by the way, I highly recommend an 11-minute, four- or eight-handed massage).

We named the gatherings "Massage Party" (how we came up with that phrase, I just cannot remember) and, as word spread, we began attracting people whose vocations were not that of massage - nurses, doctors, social workers, yoga teachers, and holistic healers. Even my regulars at MercBar, the now-defunct SoHo nightspot where I tended bar for years, eventually caught wind of my Massage Parties and teased me incessantly to create for them an event that they could attend: something less intimidating, without all the licensed massage therapists in attendance.

So, on that Leap Year's Day in 2004, during the umpteenth round of ball-busting, "When are you creating an event for us?" wheedling, I made this retort: "If Massage Party is too scary for you babies, why don't you grab your pajamas and blankies and come to my house, and I'll throw you a Cuddle Party." *Holy crap!* - I thought to myself - *A Cuddle Party? We can have Cuddle Parties!*

When I got home that night after tending bar, the entire concept and the rules of Cuddle Party poured out of me onto paper. It was as if

I was channeling the words and design. It was like a Massage Party but different. Forty minutes later, I was done. In fact, 95% of what you read on Cuddle Party's website today - the rules, the design, all of it - was captured that night. When I looked over what I had just written, I was scared shitless. Sure, I'd taught hundreds of martial arts classes and run several dozen Massage Parties, but this event was different. It felt more powerful. And I was scared.

Luckily, I was newly in love with a woman from California who was visiting in two weeks. After shyly sharing the Cuddle Party idea with her, she said it sounded awesome and that she would totally come to a Cuddle Party if I threw one. Holding it because I wanted to impress her might not have been the most enlightened intention from which to birth Cuddle Party, but that's how it happened. And am I glad I did it, because Cuddle Party was about to change my life forever.

The first Cuddle Party went so well that I held a second one a week later. Good friend Marcia Baczynski was in attendance and she immediately signed on to help me run more. Luckily for us, Marcia was a website maven and coded the entire Cuddle Party website in HTML in a single weekend. I say we were lucky because neither of us suspected what was about to happen.

Unwittingly, Marcia and I had nuzzled up to the perfect human-interest story: *New Yorkers were paying money to cuddle!* Our unique workshop taught men and women the communication skills to create safe spaces for themselves, and how to invite others into their safe spaces for non-sexual affection and welcomed touch, a.k.a. *cuddling* - a particular recipe for intimacy. And this small, publicized-just-to-friends workshop with a brand new, three-page website was about to grow bigger than we'd ever imagined.

A friend of Marcia's who was a blogger (back when blogging was the new thing) wrote about her Cuddle Party experience. Gawker.com discovered the post and humorously broke the news story, hailing Cuddle Party as proof that the Apocalypse was near. Then the media and everyone else checked out the website as pop culture swarmed upon us. The phone started ringing and didn't stop for years.

Cuddle Party was the butt of morning radio shock-jocks' rants the world over. The phone ringing at 4:30 a.m. announcing that we were "live and on the air" in Scotland or Spain was par for the course. Stephen Colbert wagged his righteously conservative and humorous finger at us from his Comedy Central pulpit on *The Colbert Report. Saturday Night Live's* hugely popular *Weekend Update* mentioned us. Jay Leno made jokes about Cuddle Party two nights in a row during his opening monologue on *The Tonight Show.* I even auditioned for the role of "Cuddle Party facilitator" on the popular crime drama, *CSI: New York,* when they wrote Cuddle Party into a murder mystery. Fortunately, the facilitator was innocent. Unfortunately, I didn't get the role. I guess I wasn't believable enough!

Yes, Cuddle Party had touched a nerve (pardon the pun) in the zeitgeist's conversation about the drawbacks of our ever-growing, digital over-connectedness in a world with less and less in-person, touchy-feely affection.

In those first two years, Marcia and I ran one to three Cuddle Parties a week to sate the media attention we were garnering. But more importantly, we were also trying to understand what our cuddlers were getting out of our chaste but humorous communication and intimacy workshop focused on non-sexual affection. The blessing of launching Cuddle Party in New York City was that people from all over the world and all walks of life attended. As long as they were at least 18 years old and abided by the rules, they were welcome to join us. We reserved the right to occasionally ask some to leave, but all were welcome to show up.

From bicycle messengers to millionaire entrepreneurs, lawyers and doctors to firemen and schoolteachers, professional dog-walkers to movie stars - they all came for different reasons:

- A Marine fresh back from war was looking to re-acclimate to civilian life.
- A single mom sought adult conversation and non-grabby kids.
- An über-straight college student wanted to listen to everyone's heartbeat during the party, men included.
- A rape survivor wanted to reclaim cuddling with men as something safe.
- An Orthodox rabbi had not been touched since his wife passed away, a decade previously.

To this day, it's still hard to say exactly *what* Cuddle Party gives people, but its impact, as you'll discover with Monique, is life-changing.

We eventually had to train and certify people to run Cuddle Parties. I credit Marcia with leading the training and certification charge that allowed Cuddle Party to thrive in four languages, and to touch thousands upon thousands of lives. To date, more than 40,000 men and women have attended Cuddle Parties worldwide. This book is a direct result of what got set in motion that Leap Year's Day in 2004, and a direct result of Monique Darling's signing up to become a certified Cuddle Party facilitator. But I'll let her tell that part of the story.

The Rules – and Monique

As for me, the rules of Cuddle Party have always been simple and direct. Yet, a decade and more than 375 personally-led Cuddle Parties later, I found myself ignoring my own advice and saying "hell yes!" to Monique's invitation. Why? It's simple, really. You *want* to say "hell yes" to Monique. You want to see the look on her face when she gets a green light to whatever crazy scheme she's just dreamt up, and you want to feel the avalanche of Monique-excitement as it cascades over you, knowing that you'll eventually read the Facebook posts and email shares from those lives Monique will touch as her enthusiasm ripples out through entire communities and to lone individuals.

Monique is the first person to write an entire book about Cuddle Party and the rules of cuddling. The rules of cuddling remain virtually unchanged with the exception of Rule #7, which originally was "NO DRY HUMPING" in all caps. We even had coffee mugs and t-shirts printed with "Rule #7 – NO DRY HUMPING!" They're collector's items today.

Rule #7 was there so people could understand where we drew the line between sexual and non-sexual. However, we eventually learned from our Cuddle Party facilitators that some of their attendees had shared that they were initially frightened to attend because they thought we had a "dry humping problem," hence, the reason we needed to have a rule (one IN ALL CAPS no less) forbidding it. Marcia and I promptly adjusted the rules, and attendance at Cuddle Parties rose a tad. I will be forever grateful that Marcia urged us to start training and certifying people to run Cuddle Parties! It gave us a perspective and reach that we never could have accessed otherwise.

For the record: just because we took out the "no dry humping" rule didn't create a frottage epidemic. (*Frottage* is the proper, fancy term for dry humping. Oh, the things you learn when you create a workshop that focuses on touch, intimacy, and affection.) Also of import to know: the rules of Cuddle Party are used today at events where dry humping, and even wet humping, are allowed. I officially left Cuddle Party in 2009 to pursue more sexually focused education. I left my baby in the capable and hug-o-licious arms of Marcia, along with an official board of Cuddle Party facilitators, so as not to confuse folks (and the media) that New York's Godfather of Cuddle was touring the country teaching safer sex workshops. Cuddle Party remains - and always will be - a non-sexual event; however, Cuddle Party's rules are 99.9% *the exact same rules* I advocate that people also use for negotiating situations that run the range from sensual to sexually explicit.

As you're about to discover, the rules of Cuddle Party are rules for life. It's fitting that the first book on Cuddle Party isn't authored by Marcia or me. If you are the founder of something, you will never experience, or fully understand, what it's like to stumble onto and interact with your creation for the first time. If you're good at what you do, you get to watch your participants have an "aha" moment or two during your workshop. If they come back again and again (if you're lucky) you can see their progress as they apply your advice - or you may have your own "aha" moment because *they* are generous enough to articulate what they got from your work in an acknowledgement or an articulate testimonial. Maybe - if you're really, really fortunate - you get to stay in touch with them for many years, and watch them integrate your work and apply it in ways you never saw anyone do before - harnessing it as they simultaneously make it their own, putting their own spin on it; passing it on to their communities, their children and families.

There's an old Bushido quote that goes, "A master isn't the one who has the most students; a master is the one who makes the most masters." As you're about to read, Monique's journey since her first Cuddle Party 'til now has been one of mastery, and I've had the great privilege of witnessing it up close and personal. Monique is an excellent example of what's possible when you take the rules of Cuddle Party and compassionately and diligently apply them to your life until they become second nature. At this point in her career, I can say Monique Darling has cuddled more people than I have (which is saying something!) and I have no doubt she will leave a flannel-clad legacy of masters in her wake. Perhaps this book will set in motion, for you, what Cuddle Party set in motion for Monique so many years ago.

Yes, I'm guilty of breaking my own, favorite Rule #5. But when it comes to Monique Darling (can you believe that her last name is *actually* Darling?) I've always been a huge "hell yes!" to watching her grow into the being she was destined to become. I suspect that my "maybe" with Monique is less a matter of disregarding my own advice, and more like The Powers That Be telling me, *"Maybe you need to model yourself after Monique now, Reid."*

So, it is with gladness and much, much pride that I introduce this book and the author that you're about to snuggle up next to. She is a master at what she does, and we need a world filled with more masters like Monique! The idea and design of Cuddle Party may have come "through me," but it's Monique Darling who has carried the flannel flag across the experiential divide and into book form.

If this book is only a fraction of what it's like to experience Monique in person, then I guarantee that what you're about to read will continue to touch your life and inspire you to dispel your fears about non-sexual, affectionate touch, find your words to ask for what you want, and especially your "hell yes!" even when you're standing at "maybe." Monique embodies what Cuddle Party is all about and why it exists, so I'm going to quietly bow out and let her tell her story. That's what I'm a "hell yes!" to. Enjoy, and Cuddle On!

Cuddle or Die
(by Kai Karrel)

There was just something about her. A light shining through. A spotlight illuminating a darkened room. Monique and I met at a conference in Times Square, New York City. She stepped into one of my classes and, before I knew it, we both stepped onto an incredible journey of the deepest friendship and growth I have ever known.

During the next couple of years, Monique and I got to travel and teach all over the United States. We both stand for truth, self-exploration, understanding the unexpressed, and revealing that which cannot be spoken. We are obsessed with finding ways to touch and express our hearts in such a profound way that every moment, every gesture is nothing but a transparent manifestation of our art, our song, our voice, our utter acceptance of who we are, to ourselves and to others.

It was quickly apparent we hold complementary gifts for one another. I'm a mystic, living most of my life in ashrams and monasteries, being taught the realm of within, mastering the path inwards. Silence, meditation, and prayer are my ways. A full and utter acceptance of all that I am, an unseen world of magnificence and brilliance. I used to see mysticism, life, love, and connection as an inside job. As happy and content as I believed I was, I was lacking one major component: the way out, the tools and ways of interacting with "Other". I was so far gone into the deep, I could hardly reach out and connect on the surface. Years of training in silence and discipline had left me somewhat crippled. I lost my ability to communicate transparently, fully, with tears and emotion.

However, the closer I got to Monique, the more apparent it became that she has mastered the outer but had yet to hear the calling back home, into the heart of hearts, back within and into her spirit. At the time, Monique was a master of communication in almost every way. I listened to her talk, connect, hug, and embrace; I watched her interactions with lovers and friends, and was utterly amazed to see a miraculous being who was able to illuminate the hearts of anyone who came her way. Yet, something was amiss. There was another layer of disconnect, of fear - a "crazy" inner dialog I saw taking place. Somehow, I realized, she was offering infinite amounts of love outwardly - caring, giving - but the inner direction was missed. She couldn't offer the same infinite attention back to herself.

It became apparent we are each other's medicine: my inner seed of acceptance and her outer blossom of connection and intimacy. The more time we spent with each other, the more affected we were by the other's presence. Together we healed my fears of connection and reclaiming my boundaries and her inability to look within and journey on her own.

Monique invited me to my first Cuddle Party. I was a hesitant "yes." What if I didn't want to cuddle someone? I had been trained to always say "yes," to "break" my ego and do the "spiritually correct thing," to put my own needs and wants aside and allow only the others to guide and direct what would occur. What if, as I had been trained, I couldn't say "no"? I remember, as I sat next to Monique, wearing my pajamas and listening to her story and the Cuddle Party rules, that a warm, fuzzy feeling of ease started flowing through me. I realized that everyone there was as uncomfortable as I was.

I will never forget her words that hit me like a lightning bolt: "'No' is a complete sentence."

The ability to set boundaries, without any excuse, without an unavoidable feeling of guilt, was a revelation. An epiphany. Something I had never heard of or considered. "If you are a 'maybe,' say 'no,'" she continued. That was it: the magic spell that set me free of years of bondage, of slavery, of "should have" and "ought to," of forgotten "maybes" and so many unexpressed "nos."

I realized that what was happening in this workshop, this Cuddle Party, was way bigger than a group of adults in their pajamas. These were the missing tools I was waiting for to connect with grace and compassion. For too many years, out of fear, I was an ostrich. I kept my head in the sand, mumbled a hesitant "yes," and lived in the shadow of guilt and shame. All I could do was hold back what I truly felt, for as long as I could, until sadly, eventually, that which wasn't expressed was expressed inappropriately. Eventually, my feelings and hidden skeletons came out in anger.

Monique opened my eyes to see there are other ways to express your needs, desires, and boundaries. There are ways to connect without so much emotional charge. There are so many other forms of interaction and communication.

I brought Monique to be my helper in a magical event I've been holding called the Goddess Puja. It is a Tantric ceremony where men and women get the opportunity to adore, worship, and offer unconditional love to one another. The puja is a non-verbal experience. It's a sacred space for a different kind of interaction: a connection of heart, and not so much of mind. I will never forget seeing the tears roll off Monique's face when she experienced this for the first time. I realized that I, too, had something profound to share with her: an opening to an inner journey that would transform her heart as much as it did mine.

Without knowing, the puja brought one of the Cuddle Party rules to life like no other: "All emotions are welcome here." The message of seeing men and women cry, laugh, shake, and burst with joy was loud and clear, knowing that this experience is the inner healing our relationships need: first inwardly, with ourselves, and then outwardly with one another.

As for Monique, the speed with which she was absorbing my teachings made way for her to embrace my mystical invitation to soar inwards. As her teachings were my missing piece, so were mine for her final ascent. Watching her soar inwardly as courageously as she does outwardly has been one of the most inspiring experiences I've had as a spiritual teacher. For a mystic, there's nothing more exciting than to witness the heart of an artist, someone who paints with their spirit the souls of so many others.

Monique has accompanied me on hundreds of pujas; we have taught and experienced the opening of hearts in Cuddle Parties, pujas, and numerous classes that encompass self-love, self-acceptance, connection, and compassion. We have been teaching communication, transparency, and sharing of truth all over the world. Our combined message is of the acknowledgement of our imperfect, perfect selves and the encouragement to live life fully, unashamed, unedited, and unfiltered.

In all my years of spiritual growth and teaching, I have never met a spiritual seeker as incredible, courageous, and bold as Monique Darling. Monique is a spirit bird, soaring the infinite skies of truth. Her feathers are made of pure love, her song is of forgotten worlds, and her wings envelope everyone she meets. It is my absolute pleasure and deepest honor to offer these words as a prelude to this incredible book. For I know that if you open your heart and allow her words to touch you, my friend, you will be taken on a journey of a lifetime.

With Love, in Love, for Love,
Kai Karrel

Interruption

Throughout this work there are many places where Monique sought out the words and knowledge of others to enhance her own, and to make sure she was on the right track. Due to the confusing subjective nature of intellectual property laws we were unable to include all of the sources that had such a profound impact on her in their entirety. For this reason a website has been created where the excerpts and additions can be found and expounded on as well as links to the source material (or as close as we can get). The website is **www.beyondcuddleparty.com** and it will be referenced throughout this book wherever there is more material she would like to share.

Introduction

Come closer as I share the intimate details of my story, then invite you along for the ride - a ride that, if you let it, will leave you transformed. Your life, and your relationships - beginning with the most important one, your relationship with yourself - will be uplifted and enhanced beyond anything you could ever imagine. Buckle your seatbelts! Keep your arms and legs inside the vehicle the whole time and prepare to never be the same.

What is Cuddle Party? And how does one become introduced, involved, in love, and passionate about it? Cuddle Party is a nonsexual event that offers participants an opportunity to experience personal exploration and intimacy with like-minded individuals, in a relaxed environment that teaches and models personal boundaries, and where a professional, appropriate atmosphere is maintained at all times. At Cuddle Parties, everyone is encouraged to engage in communication and touch, in a nonthreatening, share-affirming format.

Cuddle Party is a holistic social environment that attracts fascinating people from all walks of life and all ethnic backgrounds - from the "new adult" to the "sassy silver foxes." It provides a special and unique opportunity for connection, learning, and growth.

The event begins with a 45-minute Welcome Circle, where everyone is introduced to the "rules of cuddling," which, as you read further, might also be "rules for living."

Let me take you back to 2006 to answer what Cuddle Party means to *me*: I was one of the few sober adults who attended fan conventions of our favorite television shows. It began with Joss Whedon and *Buffy the Vampire Slayer, Angel, Firefly*, and *Dollhouse*, but soon included many more. I helped on the autograph line of the convention and got my first taste of freedom, of permission to leave what I was *supposed* to be doing for what I *wanted* to be doing.

About a year into convention-going, I was enjoying a typical last night of the latest gathering. As one of many people from around the world, drawn together by admiration for a specific television show and its cast, writers, characters, and story, I was reveling in being part of the scene as we shared anecdotes, took pictures, and felt like we mattered. Only much later did I realize that being with these "stars" was my first form of striving for a way to be next to someone who was living their passion, their soul purpose.

By the last night, most of the stars had gone home, and many of the attendees went to after-parties in one another's hotel rooms. On this particular evening, I noticed one of the regulars, a man who had, for the past 12 months, been at every convention I had seen. He was always polite and quiet, and he stuck to the background - a "supporting character" type, whereas I was usually in the lead. For reasons I found out only much later, I was, that night, drawn to him.

The conversation began in typical fashion, going over our highlights from the weekend, travel plans for heading back home the next day, and what we had enjoyed about dinner. Then I looked at him, *really* looked at him, for the first time. His eyes met mine, and everything slowed down - in fact, time stopped.

I felt rage, despair, and the most hopelessness radiating from a human being that I had ever experienced. Perhaps he simply recognized that he was being fully seen; but for whatever reason, this big, quiet, buttoned-up man broke down in tears.

He shared his anguish, his feelings that he would always be alone, his feelings of inadequacy because he recently had to move back with his mom. About fifteen minutes in, he dropped what was, for him, the biggest bombshell of all: he had not had sex in over three years, was almost never able to "get it up" any more, and felt his life was over.

I was still very religious, yet my husband and I had such clear-cut agreements that it was easy for me to offer to go up to this man's hotel room to continue sharing what was bubbling up, so long as he understood it would be *nonsexual*. This was my first experience of holding a space for someone to feel *all* that they were feeling, to say the things that they usually held back. It became a room filled with cuddling, with touch, but more importantly, with every imaginable emotion's having a chance to be felt, so it could dissipate on its own. We spent most of the next few hours spooning on his bed, me holding him from behind, while he spoke about everything that he had never, before, felt permitted to discuss.

As he hugged me goodbye, I felt his arousal coming back online. He noticed me feeling it and smiled. I gently redirected his focus back to the celebration that it was for him, rather than a call to action.

A few days later I received a letter from him, telling me what our conversation had meant to him. The letter ended with this news: his plan had been to go home after the convention and take his own life.

But now (he wrote) he felt like he had more to live for than ever. His words touched me profoundly, and began to open a place inside me that I had closed off long ago – because it wasn't safe *for me* to share my deepest thoughts, desires, and unspeakable bits.

News of what happened spread, as he shared with friends the happy story of his rebirth. His friends, in turn, shared with their friends and, during the next few conventions, people invited me to their after-parties, asking me to create a "safe, nonsexual space where we can converse, be intimate, and decompress with one another." My own version of Cuddle Party was born.

After three conventions, those friends of friends had grown to almost 30 people in a single hotel suite! It was incredible – people were touching, cuddling, and conversing about what really mattered. In fact, two people who met there became a couple and eventually married. After I returned home to Utah, I had a message waiting on Myspace (a predecessor of Facebook) along with a four-minute news clip about "Cuddle Party highlights." The message said, "Isn't this freaky?"

As I watched people cuddling, gathering together in their pajamas, receiving permission to use their voices, I wept. I began to open to the idea that maybe there were people like me out there. I immediately followed an included web-link to CuddleParty.com, and learned that a Cuddle Party, being facilitated by someone named Reid Mihalko, one of the co-founders, was scheduled in two days. And it was set for a spot near Las Vegas, only two hours away.

I grabbed my beloved husband Nathan and showed it to him. He said, "You will never see me at a Cuddle Party, but the boys and I want to support you, and also want to make sure a bunch of weirdos don't take advantage of you. So we will drive you there, drop you off, go hang out on the strip, watch the free shows until you're finished, and then pick you up."

I was so touched, because usually he didn't want to hear anything about the "weird" things I was drawn to. I purchased pink flannel pajamas, and off we went for an adventure. I was as nervous as I was excited; I wondered what the people at the Cuddle Party would think of me. I wondered if I was dragging my family out on a long night for nothing. I wondered what it would be like to experience a whole room filled with "pajama-clad" adults. I wondered who I might "have to" cuddle with. All these thoughts, and so much more, went through my mind.

At the door I was welcomed in. The greeter handed me a name tag and asked, "Would you like a hug?" I looked into this beautiful man's eyes, so touched and, at the time, *completely blown away that he would **ask** instead of just pulling me in for a hug.*

I almost broke my rule of not crying in front of people. Instead, I said a simple "yes," and he gave me one of the greatest hugs I had ever experienced. Only much later did I understand that he was hugging from a deep fullness within; he wasn't "taking" anything from me.

I felt immediately at home. Oh, and - that greeter was Reid Mihalko.

During the Welcome Circle, Reid went over the rules of cuddling. I listened with such rapt attention; a part of me knew this was a life-changing moment. These rules and these words embodied concepts I had always sensed as true, and had always hoped to encounter but had never before given myself permission to seek out. They would later become the rules by which I live my life.

As I heard the second rule – "No one has to cuddle *anyone* at a cuddle party, *ever*" – my fear of having to do *anything* immediately began to melt away. Several other rules touched me as well, and this book is about how *each one* has affected me.

During the Welcome Circle, we introduced ourselves. For the first time in my life, I felt comfortable enough to introduce myself as a healer and empath (someone who feels what others are feeling.) As soon as the words left my mouth, I looked around the circle, expecting what I had experienced for most of my early life: ridicule, judgment, and people looking at me like I was a freak, thinking me "crazy." Instead, all I received was love, acceptance, compassion, and (most beautiful of all) *understanding*.

After the Welcome Circle, the night went by in a blur. The next several hours were filled with requests from "cuddle veterans": people who had practiced asking for what they want. I cuddled with a medical intuitive. In addition to being an empath, he can sense what is happening medically in people's bodies. We had so much in common! He gave me his card and encouraged me to call him, just to chat about how life was for those of us who grew up being *unusual*. When I got up from cuddling with him, I ran for the bathroom. Even though Rule Number Nine says, "All of our emotions are welcome," I still wasn't ready to let people see me cry.

During those ten minutes in the bathroom, I sobbed joyously, finally feeling that there was a place I belonged, that I wasn't alone; the stirrings of my long-forgotten voice emerged. I left the bathroom, hoping no one would see the residue of my tears. I spent most of the rest of the evening observing everyone. All the while, I was also taking in the concept that life could really feel this good, that in that moment there was nowhere else I would rather be.

Toward the end, I got up the courage to ask the facilitator, Reid, for a few minutes of conversation. I wasn't ready to engage in cuddling with him, but I was so curious! Reid had offered these words of wisdom in the Welcome Circle: "Everyone is capable of taking care of themselves. Even if they are disappointed, they will be just fine." The words felt like a lifeline to me, having spent my entire life taking care of others.

So I asked permission to put a question to him. He said "yes," and asked if he could hold my hand. I gave my assent and we sat up against the wall, with his sparkling blue eyes peering at me as though he was taking in the essence of who I was. I was able to hold eye contact for only a few seconds at a time. Finally, I asked, "What if there are people who are alive only because you have taken care of them?"

He said he would need more information, but his first reaction was to ask, "How can you possibly know that it was because of you that they are still alive?" I dove into a story I had never shared with another, of being often abandoned with my younger siblings when we were young, sometimes for days without food, and a few times without electricity. How I became the physical protector of my siblings, as we were physically abused from a very young age. How I, by the age of 12, was big enough to stand up and throw the belt that had been used on us into the trash. So: if I had not taken care of them, if I had been more concerned about taking care of *me*, what would have happened to *them*?

Reid was very kind; he allowed me to see the tears that pooled in his eyes as he empathized with what it must have been like for me. I believe it was because of that one action, by which I saw the proof that he cared, that I was able to hear what came out of his mouth next: "Monique, what if taking care of them only enabled them to continue to think they had to be taken care of?"

He said a lot more, before getting up to start the Closing Circle, but I was stunned. That one sentence he uttered was the beginning of an understanding inside me, that all the helping, observing, and serving others was perhaps less kind than it would be to allow them to do it themselves, to give them the opportunity to *ask* for my help if and when they wanted it. *And. It. Blew. My. Mind.*

Years later, one of my most beloved friends summed up this concept for me perfectly:

The only person to serve in this moment is you. Let your service to you spill into the rest of your world … naturally. This is in no way what much of society is asking. Many need others to serve them, because they are not aware to serve themselves. This is the cycle, and I'm inviting you to get out of it. Your beauty and empowered nature is far more valuable to this world. The bee is not in service to flower, it is just taking care of its own need. Yet the flower is serviced by this act of selfishness. This is nature. You are of nature. Smile and remember. – Shawn Roop

Nathan and the boys picked me up at the end of that Cuddle Party. Truthfully, it was hard for me to leave, but luckily Reid was coming back in two weeks. So began my love affair with Cuddle Parties.

Let's fast-forward a few years. By 2009 I had become a Cuddle Party Facilitator, which is a *huge* story in itself that I will share one day. But right now, I want to share the most validating, life-affirming Cuddle Party I ever experienced. It explains why I continue facilitating Cuddle Parties.

To understand this story, it is important to know that at the first Cuddle Party I facilitated, I added a new element that many Cuddle facilitators have borrowed: when people arrive, I have them write one word, describing how they are feeling, on a slip of paper. That slip goes into a bowl or basket that is passed around during the introductions - thus, if the bowl reaches a person named "ABC," and if ABC draws out a slip with the word "nervous" on it, they will introduce themselves by saying, "I'm ABC, and I am nervous!" This is a way for everyone to see how we are reflections of one another. We all have the same feelings, and we all have stories around those feelings.

So: one evening when I was scheduled to facilitate a Cuddle Party, I had volunteered all day at Balboa Park, in San Diego, for Earth Day. All day I had been giving hugs, and getting dehydrated and sunburned. By now I had facilitated 150 (yes, one-hundred-fifty) Cuddle Parties and, that evening, for the first time ever, I faced doubt as to whether I had it in me to function for the next few hours as a facilitator. As I felt into it, I heard a voice say, *"Go. It's important. Go!"* So I did.

I showed up exactly as I was: tired, burned, and sad. As I began to write my word, the truth of that moment was that I felt *heartbroken.* Up to that point, at all my previous 150 Cuddle Parties, my word had always been *enticing.* (As you get to know me through this book, you will see how *Monique* = *enticing* ... they go together so well.) I decided to fully walk my talk, and dropped that word in the bowl.

As it happened, we had a participant from Colorado who had never heard of Cuddle Parties until, now visiting San Diego for only two days, she had agreed to come along when her friend invited her.

Another important point: the start of the Welcome Circle marks the cut-off time for any further arrivals of participants. Since feeling safe is essential at Cuddle Party, it needs to be unquestionable that everybody is on the same page, fully informed about the Rules for the event. To let people in, after they have missed some part of the Welcome Circle and the orientation it provides, would undermine the group's confidence. However, this time a young man had called to ask if we could keep the doors open fifteen more minutes, as he had just read about it online and knew he had to be there. I took a vote from the room, and since the "yes" was unanimous, we held the doors open for him. After he arrived, ten minutes later, we locked the doors and began.

When the basket with the slips of paper got to the woman from Colorado, she reached in, looked at the paper for a moment, stated her name, then added " ... and I'm heartbroken."

Then she burst into huge sobs.

Her friend said, "This is so appropriate, as today is the exact one-year anniversary of her son's murder."

There were gasps, empathetic love, and energy-level hugs from around the room.

Then, our latecomer - the one for whom we had voted to hold the doors open - asked her, "Is your son's name ... ?"

She stood. He stood. They ran to the center of the room and collapsed into each other's arms. We soon learned that he had been her son's best friend growing up.

That was the most vulnerable, heartfelt, connective Cuddle Party I have ever attended. It solidified, for me, the certainty that there is a reason that each and every person walks through the door for any particular event. There are millions of people in San Diego, and yet those were the ones who said, "yes" that night.

I have witnessed similar experiences at almost every Cuddle Party I have ever facilitated or attended. People connect, something is said in a way it has never been said before, lives are changed and transformed forever - all because there is a space, a container for people to come as they are and be who they are.

That is why Cuddle Party means so much to me. Now I will take you through the rules of Cuddle Parties, laying them out one by one and offering you the wisdom they have given me. Then I will invite you to play with them as "life rules" with some simple exercises to bring those points home.

Are you ready?

Rule #1: Pajamas Stay on the Whole Time

"It's easy to take off your clothes and have sex. People do it all the time. But opening up your soul to someone, letting them into your spirit, thoughts, fears, future, hopes, dreams ... that is being naked."
– Rob Bell

Cuddle Parties are all about depth, communication, connection, and play. They are completely non-sexual, and the first step towards keeping it that way is to make sure that clothing remains on. What I love about this rule is that the container it creates is one that many (if not most) people *never* get to experience in their lifetime: a place where touch, consent, and connection are all happening without the possibility of sex entering in.

Many of us equate touch - especially cuddling - with sex, so what happens when we open that equation up? What I have experienced is a higher level of trust, a greater depth of connection, more meaningful conversations, and just touching because touch feels good. All the stories of, "If I do this, will he think I mean I'm okay with that?" or "Will she take my flirting to mean I now want to sleep with her?" or defaulting to old standby routines start to disappear. Instead, you are more able to be in this moment, feeling exactly what is happening to you. Everything begins to slow down; you are more aware of your breath, of the hairs on your arms, of what you are not asking for, of what you no longer need to hide - because you have your clothing as a shield. In an unanticipated way, the fact that you "can't" get naked leaves you free to explore every other level of your "bare" self.

> *The moment that you feel, just possibly, you are walking down the street naked, exposing too much of your heart and your mind, and what exists on the inside, showing too much of yourself … that is the moment you might be starting to get it right.* – Neil Gaiman

The most touching example of what Neil is referring to was when I got a front-row seat to an amazingly courageous woman's experience. The Cuddle Party she came to was lot like any other Cuddle Party, but for her it was one of the biggest steps, and gifts, she had ever allowed herself. She showed up that Sunday night - timid, tearful, with one foot in the door but most of her body ready to bolt at any sudden movement. She declined my hug of greeting, and looked utterly stunned when I offered back, "Thank you for taking care of yourself," with a smile. I helped her get comfortable in her own corner so she had room to observe without having her space impinged upon. I asked her if she was willing to share one anxiety with me, because often if we can give our fears a voice, they seem *much* less scary. She looked at me as if I were a cross between a long-hoped-for lifeline and an alien from the farthest planet she could imagine. For a moment I thought she was going to answer, because her eyes became a little less guarded; but then she clamped her lips tighter and shook her head.

During the Welcome Circle, as we went around the room introducing ourselves, she said her name, and shared her word from the bowl of words that we all choose from: *anxious* (so relevant, as the words usually are.) Again it looked like she had a lot more to say, but instead she put her head down and passed the bowl to the next attendee.

As I went through the rules that night, I paid particular attention to this woman. At times she was captivated, eyes glued to mine; at times she just sat there silently sobbing. Other times she seemed completely distracted, not even in the room at all. As we came to the last exercise in the Welcome Circle, which is done in groups of three, she got up and sat next to me. I usually don't participate in the ice-breakers, but felt this would be a good occasion for a "powerful exception."

I invited everyone to join a triad, and led them into a rich negotiating experience: in one round, everyone gets to say "no" to everything, in another they get to say "yes" to everything (not actually doing it), and in the final round they get to offer what they would *love* to do with the other two people in their group. Then they negotiate, from the combination of everyone's desires in the group. They keep negotiating until everyone is a "hell yes," and then they get to do that activity.

After I had turned them loose to request, negotiate, and experience their little groups, I turned all my attention to the woman next to me. She began by asking if she could touch my leg with her leg. I said, "yes," giggling inside as I remembered my nervousness when first approaching Reid, all those years before. She moved very slowly and deliberately until her leg was just brushing against mine. She began talking, and once she let herself start, the words began pouring out. She shared about her childhood abuse, being ganged-raped as a teenager, and then going almost immediately into a super-violent marriage. I asked her to pause for a moment while I turned everyone else loose from their groups of three, to co-create that night's Cuddle Party, then turned back to this brave woman, leg to leg, heart to heart with me.

She was able to say all the stuff that had been bottled up inside her for years. Her story ended with her husband's passing away eight years ago, and how she had not allowed herself to be touched since, rarely even leaving her house. But when an online friend sent her a link about this Cuddle Party, something that she thought had died long ago was awakened. As scared as she was, she knew she had to attend. She eventually asked if I would spoon with her, and I said, "yes." Later she even allowed herself to be a sandwich in a three-person snuggle.

During the Closing Circle, I opened the floor for "aha" moments, challenges, gratitude's, and anything else that people wanted to express or have witnessed. This beautiful woman was able to share with the group what it had taken for her to be there that night, and how grateful she was for the feeling of hope she was leaving with, that perhaps things could be different, that she could be different. Then she made one, final request: would we be willing to find a way for everyone in the circle to put a finger on her? Just a finger, but she would like to see what that felt like. The people in the circle were a "yes," and I will never forget how radiantly her face transformed as we each laid a single finger somewhere on her body.

I absolutely believe that whole transformation could not have happened without a non-sexual container that helps liberate exploration where there is discomfort around touch and being touched.

I also love the playfulness this rule brings out when adults get to spend an afternoon or evening in their PJs. How many of us grew up going to sleepovers where we stayed up all night eating junk food, building pillow forts, playing superheroes in our pajamas, and often ended up in a big pile ("accidental cuddling")? And how, after that, our sharing would just start tumbling out? We now know that extended touch or cuddling produces the chemical oxytocin in our bodies. Oxytocin is a hormone that does everything from making you feel good to helping you feel connected to others.

"New research is suggesting that oxytocin plays a crucial role in enabling us to not just forge and strengthen our social relations, but also to stave off a number of psychological and physiological problems. But more conceptually, oxytocin is proving to be a critical ingredient to what makes us human." George Dvorsky "Eight Reasons Why Oxytocin Is the Most Amazing Molecule in the World". See all Eight Reasons at www.beyondcuddleparty.com

What a gift to be able to relive some of those childhood memories as an adult! Cuddle Parties create a container for tapping into that childlike joy, where we can touch for touch's sake, talk about anything, explore and experiment with the edge of our comfort zone, because there is an agreed-upon boundary, a mutual limit - in this case, sexuality - that is factored out of the equation. This leaves all parties free to explore right up to the threshold, in large measure because it is safe to explore when a specific boundary is offered.

As another example, take the study that was done with grade-school children playing in a schoolyard at recess. The question: What would happen if their playground fence was removed? The changes were remarkable. With the fence absent, the children huddled fearfully by the school door, or stayed together in the middle of the playground. One would imagine they would fearlessly explore the newly unbounded environment. Instead, without a fence, the children were not able to see a given boundary or limit and thus were more reluctant to leave the perceived safety of the group, the center. Without the fence they became more cautious. They drew in, and restricted their activity to the *known* structure of the playground equipment. When the fences were returned to their original place, guess what happened? The *very next day* those same children were all over the playground again, playing right up to the fence, happy and secure. Thus in a very real sense, the fence, rather than being simply an instrument of constraint, became one of liberation!

Adults, like these children, have an innate need for, and an appreciation of, structure. What happens when we begin to decide where our own "fences" lie? When we give ourselves permission to play right up to the edge, sometimes even climb up on a past "fence" to see where we want to play today?

One "fence" I always liked to climb was playing dress-up. For as long as I can remember, I have enjoyed any opportunity for the ritual and joy of trying on and selecting my clothes for some special occasion. I loved prom, school dances, and Halloween, because they gave me the excuse I thought I needed, the permission to express myself. As I started on the convention circuit, my favorite accessory was a flower in my hair. There was something fulfilling about getting to be "fancy," even in a small way. When I began going to workshops, it was a fantastic excuse to dress up: to wear flowers, exotic dresses, leggings with slits cut out, and other things that made me feel sexy. But I would have never dared to wear my special selections if I hadn't given myself the permission that arose from the fact that I was going to a workshop.

At one particular workshop, the facilitator, Lawrence Lanoff, was a good friend of mine; I admired and was quite attracted to him. On the second-to-last day he said to me, "Monique, I appreciate the extra time you take to make yourself feel good, by looking so good." He looked me up and down and let me see his appreciation, then moved back into facilitator mode. Sadly, at the time, I thought he was mocking me, or even worse, that he thought I was pathetic – after all, since he noticed me dressing up, he *must* think I was doing it only for him, to impress and entice him! In actuality, his appreciation was just a side benefit, because I dressed up for myself, so I could show up as confidently as I was able to. I was still super trapped in many of my own insecurities that boiled down to this core issue: I had to prove my right to exist.

Forward, six months, to New Year's Eve: I was texting this same facilitator, who was now - besides a friend - a collaborator and deep love of mine. It dawned on me what he had meant, all those months ago. He had been appreciating me *for* giving myself permission to dress up for me. It was my joy in my own beauty that brightened up the room, and made it a gift for him and everyone else there. I couldn't wait to share this realization with him. He sent back a smiley face and agreed – I got it! From that moment, it was like some unseen shackles were dropped, some hidden voices were silenced, and I began dressing in outrageous ways, wearing "costumes" of my own design, leg warmers on my arms, furry pants, fairy princess dresses, and more. Just because it brought me joy. So as I walked around in my own personal design, every moment was a fantastic one because I was doing something I loved, and I was accepting and offering myself to the world.

How does this transfer to Cuddle Party? Well, I had started out always bringing my PJs in a bag, and changing when I got to the party. But as I grew more comfortable in my own skin, and in wearing more of my "insides" on my outsides, I began wearing my pajamas in the car, then in the store before the car … and then sometimes I wore them all day, everywhere I went, just because I could!

I remember the first time I dared to wear my pajamas in public. I had just attended a Cuddle Party at Reid's loft in Oakland, and the next day I was still wearing my PJs as I hopped into my little red rental car and onto the I-5 to drive home to San Diego. With the windows down, I was rocking out, moving and singing with my favorite songs. There was another car that kept driving up close behind me. When I slowed down and moved over to the right, that car slowed down and drove up next to mine, *on the shoulder of the freeway*! I finally turned to see what they could possibly want. It was a very cute man who had written his number on a sheet of paper and was holding it up while he was driving, inviting me to call him.

I laughed, still not believing this was actually happening, and dialed his number.

We flirted back and forth, by phone, for the next 20 minutes, until we decided to stop for lunch. He was a beautiful Italian actor from LA, and my carefree-dancing, pajama-wearing ways had enticed him to want to get to know me better. That experience began to open my mind to do things, to wear things, to be myself because it made *me* happy, regardless of what anyone else thought.

EXERCISES FOR RULE #1

1. Create a container with your partner, one in which sex is off the table for an extended amount of time. You can negotiate on the time period: it can be an hour, a day, or a week. The duration doesn't matter as much as what you explore within the time that is set. I invite you to explore the possibilities when sex is not part of the equation. (As always, you decide what defines "sex" for you! Is it intercourse? Second base? Heavy kissing?) Once you have established where your boundary is for this time together, then relax, have fun, and begin playing. Start to notice where you feel more free, where you may want to explore touch, conversation; maybe ask for that massage or hair-washing you have not found time to do together. Allow your imaginations to go wild! One suggestion that makes it even more playful: each of you write seven to ten things that fall within the parameters you have agreed on, then place them in separate bowls. Take turns picking from the other's bowl and then try these new things, or connect with them in new ways.

2. Give yourself permission to wear "costumes" in public. Wear whatever helps you feel vulnerable, beautiful, confident, and able to show up emotionally disrobed and "naked." It may be that polka dot bikini you have been waiting for an excuse to wear; it could be that formal dress you have been eyeing in the local thrift store, a flapper dress, or a furry coat. Or maybe your edge is actually wearing your pajamas outside your bedroom. The invitation is to open your imagination. Let go of caring what anyone else will think, let go of what's proper, classy, in style, or "cool," and let yourself wear on the outside how you feel on the inside.

- What if we chose to walk around "naked"? Clothing could be optional, but I am talking about a deeper *nakedness*.

- What if every decision, every interaction, every unedited word, every gesture, every touch, every step came from our own raw, naked truth/presence/yes of *this* moment?

- What if we never had to hide, what if we stopped trying to impress, what if our deepest depths *were* the greatest gift we have to offer?

- What if there was no losing, nothing to gain, no one to compete with, nothing to be taken – because we offer it *all*?

- What if it was okay to be the only one doing that?

- What if we did not need any "return"?

- What if our greatest gift to ourselves was loving and accepting ourselves *so* completely that we trust ourselves enough to walk through the world completely "naked"?

Rule #2: You Don't Have to Cuddle Anyone at a Cuddle Party Ever!

"Look to your heart and soul first, rather than looking to your head first, when choosing. Rather than what you think, consider instead how you feel. Look to the nature of things. Feel your choices and decisions. It just might change everything." – Jeffrey R. Anderson

This second rule states that there is *nothing* you must do at a Cuddle Party, except follow the rules. This opens up the entire experience, makes each event unique, and gives everyone in the room an opportunity to co-create the experience. Reid taught me early on, "The event will go how the event will go." This advice allowed me to let go of its having to be "perfect." (Is there really such a thing? Even if there were, who could possibly qualify to judge whether it was or not?)

This rule boils down to the following: we are at choice every moment when we can truly accept, own, and honor that we are choosing our lives - *our lives as the results of decisions we make* - and when we can let go of what society, religion, and our parents and teachers have told us to do (or demanded that we do). When we accept and let go in these two ways, we begin to reclaim our power and remember our inner truth: we affect the world, and we "happen" to the world, not the other way around. When we realize that nothing is happening *to* us, we begin to set ourselves free.

Some people come to Cuddle Party and sleep most of the night, some carry on in-depth conversations, some write in a journal, some can't get enough cuddles, and some practice saying "no" the entire night. At the first Cuddle Party in Utah, the closest that most attendees ever got to cuddling was when they rolled the dice for the board game they were playing: every once in a while, their elbows would brush up against each other. Guess what? They had an amazing night!

Just as Rule Number One opens up a new doorway to touch when sex is off the table, this rule opens up your mind, heart, body, and soul to the concept that there is really nothing you *have* to do, *ever*. As a result, it begins changing past patterns of sacrifice, victimhood, obligation, "have to," "should have," and even the concept of "right" or "wrong." I love the Sufi poet Rumi, and my absolute favorite quote of his is, "Out beyond ideas of wrong and right doing, there is a field. I'll meet you there."

For most of my years I lived on the edge of panic, believing, "The world is about to end." I was the first person everyone called in a crisis, because I spent so much energy thinking up every "what if" scenario I could imagine, preparing for every disaster, and being on call in case things fell apart. (The rest of my time was spent "reading" people: observing their moods, walking on eggshells, hoping to cause the least amount of trouble in their lives.) When something did go way off course, it was easy for me to keep my head because I was used to sitting with the discomfort of being out of control.

The predictable trade-off for all this hypervigilant preparedness was that I was missing out on the beauty (and connections) around me. Since my body was always on high alert, I could never relax and enjoy the *present* moment; all my energy was directed to a future moment that might or might not happen (but, by golly, I was prepared if it did.)

Cuddle Party became my laboratory, my research and development arena. There is a gift within the fact that the "container" is for a *set* amount of time, with a beginning and an end. Little by little, I learned to take my "what if" hat off at the door, knowing I could put it back on when I left.

While I was in the Cuddle Party itself, I got to practice relaxing, being with whatever I was feeling and whatever another was feeling, without having to preemptively guess.

There I began to unravel the religious teachings I was brought up with. These teachings said, "Here is your checklist. You must do these things, and then you will be rewarded when you die. These are the right things to do to get you into Heaven." Instead, I more and more used the strategy of tuning into my body whenever there was a choice. Through this added awareness, and this giving of permission to my intuition, little by little what became "right" to me was whatever felt good in my body - whichever choice offered more space inside me to be able to feel even more at any given time. That space felt like freedom to me - freedom from the barrage of "what if" voices in my head, freedom to actually love God instead of fear Him, and freedom to begin choosing to be with people. Once right versus wrong, obligation, "should," and "must" were out of the way, each interaction became a celebration. If my world was filled with limitless possibilities, why not pick exactly what I wanted to do at any moment, and then totally revel in, and savor, every second? My questioning, wondering, and agonizing over whether I was doing the "right" thing began softening as I was repeatedly shown the following: there isn't a "right" answer; freedom/liberation comes from being open to my heart, mind, spirit, and *especially* my body; and the "right" answer for me is what will bring the most joy in any given moment. I feel deep down that I have the choice, that I am not committed to anything, and do not have to do anything. Hence in that absolute freedom lies sweet joy in the full embrace/surrender/ awareness of playing in *this* moment, being exactly as I am. Here is the best part: I have much more room within my psyche when I remember that whatever the people around me are doing is "right" for them, and it's not my responsibility to change or "save" them.

I have two stories that I gratefully share, to show how I was able to respond as I did only because of the practice grounds of all those Cuddle Parties:

One early morning, I waited in a much-longer-than-usual security line at the Oakland Airport. Everyone was stressed and upset about the delay, afraid of missing their flights. A man in front of me turned around and initiated a conversation. "I'm gonna die, I'm flying to a hospital to die, and because of this stupid line, I may miss my flight," he said tersely and dramatically, then waited for my response. I just stood there, keeping his gaze, holding him exactly where he was. He looked surprised, but then got angrier and cursed the line, people, and God. He finally stopped and looked at me again.

I was still there, just being with him and feeling such gratitude for the opportunity of this "chance" encounter. After a few minutes of being the "tough guy" and expelling his rage, he began crying (great big sobs) and asked me for my name. For the rest of our wait in that long line, we talked about God, compassion, how we truly all have an expiration date, and so much more. He shared that he hadn't been able to tell his daughter what was happening to him; he just kissed her on the forehead that morning, said, "I love you," then drove away. He kept thanking me for being so kind, and I kept thanking him for giving me the gift of remembering how precious each breath is. We stood for a few minutes, breathing together, appreciating the magnificence and true gift of a single breath, a moment of connection.

When he finally made it through security and ran for his flight, the last words out of his mouth were, "When I reach the other side, the first thing I will say is 'thank you' to God for Monique." The rest of the journey to my plane was filled with such tenderness; I was sobbing in gratitude and couldn't wait to tell my sons how much I loved them.

I am grateful for the gift of being with people, almost every day, in workshop-space. I even get to direct them in an exercise, during my silent puja, of meeting themselves on their death beds and feeling the preciousness of life. And yet that day I got to experience this so directly that it was one of the most holy moments I could ever imagine. I appreciate the gift of that man that morning, the gift of the awareness that we have an expiration date for this life. "This too shall pass" ... so what is there to do but choose to fully feel/experience each moment!

The second story, oddly enough, also occurred in an airport, and what follows is from my Facebook post that day:

There aren't words for the gratitude that is flowing through my veins. People have said to me before that I live my life as a teaching versus being a teacher. But I have never truly felt that way towards myself until this moment!

I'm sitting on a flight with people irate and upset, angry all around me because our flight is delayed for maintenance issues. Yet I am calm as I sit here in such joy with tears pouring down my face, listening to my favorite meditation music and offering much devotion and appreciation to the universe for just this moment!

Because the flight was delayed I was available for a call from Nathan. My sons tentatively asked if they could please stay home and go to a party and not pick me up at the airport. This was super brave to ask, as they were already feeling defeated and that it was highly unlikely I would say yes. Even a few months ago I would have taken it personally, so desiring for them to want to pick me!

But as Nathan asked me, all I was filled with was gratitude that they can give me room to grow, that they would ask something and be open to me giving a new (different) answer than I have always given. As I felt how happy I was that they were taking care of themselves, a part of me wished they wanted to meet me at the airport more than go to a party; but it no longer means anything about me, so when they do say yes it will be such an authentic celebration. I love them so much! I love that pieces of what I offer to the world have finally helped shift me.

I was talking with a friend yesterday, and he was commenting how powerful anger can feel, but can I be available to feel what's underneath, allow my grief, my feelings to come and go so I can be available for the subtle beauty of this moment? I have never felt more open or more grateful. I long for connection so greatly, and the best way to meet and honor that desire is to be open to connecting to myself, honoring every aspect, loving and accepting every piece, letting go of 'right' or 'wrong' so I am here.

As I finish typing this, the maintenance guy just fixed the door; none of the fear, anger, and upset made it go any faster. Because my first 'go to' was not that, I was here with all this beauty and was able to share it with you.

Tonight, as I hold my boys, I'm home. But you know what? On this plane, with my music and tears, I am already home.

My sons went to their party that night. The plane I transferred to also had mechanical issues – in fact, this time we had to get off and wait for a new plane. By the time I landed in Utah, it was late enough that my boys had finished their party and were waiting at the baggage carousel to hug and welcome me. Had I not been able to feel into their question, without a forgone, set conclusion, we would have all lost: they would have missed their party, and the flight delays would have felt horrible to me because I would have felt that my inability to be flexible and my need to be "right" had left them without choice. The beauty of letting go of any way it was "supposed" to go left it open to be exactly what we all wanted.

These are two incredible examples from my life of how this second rule ("You don't have to cuddle anyone") has shifted everything for me. This rule also means you can leave a Cuddle Party at any time. If you leave right after the Welcome Circle, you get a full refund. I remember a shy, timid man who attended a Cuddle Party a few years ago. After hearing Rule Number Two, he abruptly stood up and walked out of the space. Many other attendees approached me during the cuddling, clearly worried about him. They wanted to know what happened, if there was anything I could have done to get him to stay, and if there was anything I was going to do to follow up.

I loved the conversations his choice opened up. A lot of my cuddle veterans were still spending most of their lives trying to take care of others. This was a great opportunity for them to see that pattern and begin letting go of another's experience. I did try to follow up with that gentleman but did not get a reply, so I let it go.

About a year later, the same man walked into another Cuddle Party I was facilitating. He made it through the Welcome Circle and then requested some time for a conversation. I was a solid "yes"; what he shared touched me deeply. He said that since that first Cuddle Party, where he felt so overwhelmed he had to leave, he had come to several other Cuddle Parties. I was surprised, because I did not remember ever seeing him again until this night. He giggled nervously and said that at the ones after that first one, he had sat in his car, walked halfway up the driveway, and even made it all the way to the doorway for one. But each time he had chickened out and left without coming inside. He felt awkward and embarrassed about having left so abruptly that first time.

I asked him if I could share what happened after he left that night; he was a "yes," so I told him that he had been a great teacher for so many in the room, including myself, for all the parts of us that still want to take care of someone else, that are still stuck in the belief that there is a "right" way for everything to go. I thanked him for his gift that night, and this quiet, shy man first began to cry and then proceeded to light up like a Christmas tree. As the light switched on in his head, I could see his realization that there is nothing he has to do at a Cuddle Party ever, which in turn could open up into how there is nothing he has to do in life, *ever.*

EXERCISES FOR RULE #2

1. Make a list of everything you feel you *have* to do daily, weekly, or monthly. Write what would happen if you did not do them. Let yourself feel into all the "disasters" that would occur. Then begin opening to the possibility that you do not have to do any of them. Feel how that resonates in your body. Then begin creating containers where you can practice letting go of your own "have to's," "should haves," and "right/wrong" ways of doing things. Even if it is only for 10 minutes, you will begin building muscles, creating new reference points for a world where the things you do are what you desire to do. Even if you are doing things that are less than your ideal, you can do them from a more joyous place – *because instead of its happening to you, you are choosing, and therefore you are "happening" to it.*

2. I invite you to take something you feel strongly about – a belief or value. Close your eyes and consider a belief or value you feel strongly about, enough that you would defend it. Allow yourself to feel it throughout your body. What does it feel like to have such conviction? Stay there a few minutes, just feeling it. Now that you have allowed yourself to feel into how deeply you believe this thing, breathe and take the exact opposite position; play devil's advocate for a few minutes. Find a place inside that feels just as powerful defending the opposite side as you did a minute ago defending what you value as "right." Now take another breath and see how it feels to let go of both. Every argument for anything has at least as many arguments against it. When we can create more space to be able to feel anywhere along the spectrum, "right versus wrong" and "good versus bad" drop away. Our values become flexible, once more coming back to "nothing has to be done, ever." Which brings us right back to acting from choice.

Rule #3: You Must Ask Permission and Receive a Verbal "Yes" Before You Touch Anyone

"Silence isn't golden, and it surely doesn't mean consent, so start practicing the art of communication." – TD Jakes

"Consent is not the absence of a no; it is the presence of a yes.

Consent is given, not taken.

Consent is active, not passive.

Consent is not implied. Consent cannot be assumed.

Consent is always necessary, and its absence is inexcusable."

– ERIN RIORDAN

Rule Number Three is all about consent and asking a different type of question. You must ask for something you would like, and get a verbal "yes." Or someone asks you for something they would like, and you agree to it. Some of my favorite ways to start:

- Begin with something easy: ask to hold someone's hand, or begin with a conversation, finding a subject that delights you both.

- Start with your most bold request: for example, ask the one person in the room who makes your heart pitter-patter for that one thing you would really like, that feels "too good," that totally pushes your comfort zone - because regardless of what they answer, any request after that will be a piece of cake.

- Start with the scariest, most awkward request (as Reid instructs, "Walk toward the gun" instead of running away or avoiding it). Then be as specific as possible – as examples, rather than "Can we talk?" or "May I touch you?" or "Would you get me a sundae?" ask for a 30-minute conversation, a lower-back rub, a sundae with chocolate peanut butter topping with whipped cream and a cherry. By being specific, it gives the person you are asking a much clearer request from which they can find their internal yes or no.

Another vital part of this rule states, "If you do get a 'no' (silent or otherwise), don't take it personally. It just means someone else is being true to themselves. Hearing a 'no' doesn't mean you asked for the wrong thing or that there is something wrong with you." Throughout this chapter, toy with the idea that there is no such thing as *rejection*. Instead, think about this: what if rejection = redirection? Steve Maraboli says, "As I look back on my life, I realize that every time I thought I was being rejected from something good, I was actually being redirected to something better." How does that feel inside? Stop reading, close your eyes, and take a breath. How much more space can you make within by just considering this concept? Accepting rejection is part of embracing the uncertainty of life. *It can be beautiful to not know!*

Asking for what we want can be challenging. Those little voices and experiences from our past can take a fully-realized adult right back into that awkward, risky place of adolescence. For me, it was Michael (not his real name). I had the biggest crush on him the whole year of seventh grade. Then, for the last school dance before summer, I wore a pink dress my grandma bought me and a pink bow in my hair. My favorite slow song came on. I cautiously made my way to the group of kids where Michael was hanging out, gently tapped him on the shoulder, and asked, "Would you like to dance?" He turned, looked at me, and then turned back around to resume his conversation with his friends - without a word to me. My heart breaking, and feeling sure the entire world could see what a loser I was, I walked back across the gym floor and continued out the door, filled with shame and never wanting to risk asking for anything ever again!

Eventually I did ask again, but I spent the next 20 years living by this policy: do everything in my power to be nice and loveable, to please people and serve them, to give those around me a reason to say "yes." (The catch-22 was that subconsciously I could never trust another's "yes" until they could give me an honest "no.")

For a glimpse of how many things I was trying to be a "yes" to, picture this: My husband and I had a sister who lived with me from the time she was 18, a brother who lived with us off and on from the time he was 12, and another sister whom Nathan and I took in after she became a ward of the state. I was still constantly seeking approval from Mom and Dad and drove 60 minutes a day to see my Grandma, bringing my sons (aged two, five, and twelve) to spend time with her. I also held a high position in our church, which took lots of hours.

Ironically, my job in a nutrition store was about helping people become healthier. My boss was a beautiful man who had held the "Mr. Utah" bodybuilding title. Our body-conscious customers included many bodybuilders, and I too was getting up at 4 a.m. to work out with my boss, send the boys off to school, and then head off to work - only to return home to cook, clean, and help with homework. And because I longed for personal connection, I constantly had friends over, gave massages, and searched for ways to add value to everyone's life. I put so much pressure on myself to find a way to be a "yes"!

All that craziness came to a head one Thanksgiving. I had created a magnificent feast for my mom, siblings, husband, sons, and a few friends and neighbors. I had cooked, cleaned, and hosted, all the while feeling that I was coming down with something, for I had a headache, fever, and chills. But I carried on with Dayquil and basked in how awesome everyone thought I was.

The other manager had called in sick for work the next day, so my boss was counting on me to help him with the huge after-holiday sale. At one time, the two of us had 30 customers at once. In between helping people find what they wanted, and working the cash register, I was in the bathroom throwing up, and alternating between Dayquil, Tylenol, ibuprofen, aspirin, and cough drops to try to keep my fever down and my cough managed enough that no one would know I was sick.

I made it to closing time. Nathan was on his way to pick me up and I was shivering uncontrollably. I waited outside so my boss wouldn't know I had been sick all day. I didn't want anyone to see me as weak or not valuable. As Nathan pulled up, I began sobbing. He took me to the ER. With a temperature of 103.5 degrees, I had: a sinus infection, kidney stones, the beginning of pneumonia, and some virus that was going around. They kept me overnight, pumping me full of fluids and antibiotics; meanwhile, I begged Nathan to cover for me with work, family, and church so none of them would know how sick I was and worry about me.

It seems unreal, now. I have so much compassion for that scared Monique who needed everyone to love her so much that she continued saying "yes" long after she had become a "no."

Today, I so appreciate the courage of a beloved (whether they are my kin, or one of those I am honored to be relating with) who says "no" when they are a no, and "yes" only when they are a "hell yes." I gain confidence by asking for *anything* I want, rather than censoring myself to ask only for what I think they will be a "yes" to. I have learned to trust and love myself even more as I consistently stay true to my "no's." Now I can honor hearing a "no" just as much as a "yes," and I can authentically reply, "Thank you for taking care of yourself."

Cuddle Party encourages the feeling of fearless relating. Imagine you are a child riding your tricycle on a big, expansive playground. You ride up to a group of kids and say, "Hey, anyone wanna ride on the back of my tricycle?" They all say "no." You ride up to the next group of kids and ask the same question. They, too, decline your invitation. Guess what? You will keep on inviting other kids to join you until you get a "yes" or you tire yourself out. You aren't thinking, by the second or third time, "Oh, no, is it me? Is it my tricycle? Am I the kid with *that* tricycle they talk about at lunch?" All that is what happens as we get older: after a few "no's," we begin to think it's about us, that we asked the wrong way, for the wrong thing, or there's something wrong with us, and eventually we just stop asking because it feels too risky.

I invite you to ask anyway. It feels so good inside to honor yourself this way! It becomes easier with practice, and you start reframing what it means to hear "no."

By asking before you touch, you offer a beautiful gift that is rare in our culture: the gift of voice. By asking before touching, then waiting for the other's answer, it shows that you can wholeheartedly honor a "no" just as much as you honor a "yes." You offer the other choice and voice around how their body is to be touched.

Think of the ways we are touched without our consent: Aunt Bea pinches your cheeks, your mom tells you to hug or kiss Grandpa, a co-worker pats you on the back; a date stretches his arm in a yawn, and the arm ends up resting on your shoulder. Offering the request of permission to those around you, so that they may begin feeling into, and responding with, their "yes" or "no" before allowing their bodies to be touched, is one of the most empowering tools you can help them reclaim.

This practice helps us to separate touch from sex, obligation, right, or money, and leads us toward celebrating and honoring touch for touch's sake.

As you gain new reference points for what rejection/redirection feels like inside your body, the world begins to transform in front of your eyes. You begin trusting yourself that whatever answer you give or get is the right one for you. You begin trusting that those around you, in response to *your* asking for all *you* want (your "100 percent"), will opt in or out according to their authentic choosing. This leads to a wider community versed in self-sufficiency, unedited communication, and more-frequent consent.

When those around you use their voice effectively, it leads to fewer stories and assumptions of what may be happening with the other person (stories that are usually going on only inside your own head.) One of my beloveds, Lawrence Lanoff, gives the perfect analogy on this subject: Think of an apple. What color is it? What shape? What size? Would it surprise you to know I was thinking of a heart-shaped, pink, glitter apple, about the size of a bowling ball? Try asking friends, family, colleagues - each one will have a different answer. Some may see an Apple computer;

a poisoned apple; a red, green, or yellow delicious one; it may be on the tree or in a woman's hand; it may have one, two, or three leaves, or it may have none. The ways in which that simple apple could appear in anyone's head are infinite. Even if you ask them to see the word *apple* in writing, the letters take on their own flavor for each person doing the exercise. That is an apple!

Now imagine something much more complex such as love, relationship, or consent, and realize how different they may look or feel from each person's point of view. This brings us right back to the rule: Ask! We don't know what is happening inside another, even if we have known them intimately for some time. If, by asking, you offer curiosity, wonder, and a desire to know what's currently happening inside their heart and mind, your relationship stays current, and you both have freedom to grow, shift, and change, without being held to who you used to be.

I *love* questions! "I don't judge …" is a phrase that has currency, these days. **Curiosity, to me, is the opposite of judgment.**

Another personal story: I was helping a beloved move from his New York apartment. As we packed, painted, and cleaned, he knocked over a cherished item. In his "oh no," I heard so much pain and loss, but he swept it up and wanted to keep going. Later that night, I stayed with his belongings that we had piled on the curb while he trotted across the street to pick up the car we had rented for a few hours. A few minutes later, I looked up and saw him standing on my side of the street. I thought the car must be on this side of the street after all, but then I saw that the car was not there, and that he was focused on texting. I immediately imagined that he was sharing with another beloved what had happened to his treasured item. Two or three times I began walking down the street, wanting to be a part of the conversation and to hold him in that loss, but ultimately I decided to stay with his stuff on the curb.

A few minutes later, he turned around, and I realized it wasn't him! It was a random New Yorker with a similar haircut who happened to be wearing almost identical clothes. A few moments after that realization, my beloved drove up in the car, waving and smiling hugely. As he pulled up, he must have seen something on my face, because he asked, "What?" I said, "I don't want to tell you." to which he replied, "Then you simply must."

I explained the story that had just played out in my mind, afraid he would be angry, or think I was stupid or crazy. He laughed so hard he was crying, and that began a deeper level of connecting for us that has since transferred to anyone I am relating with. When something is not being said, when there is a story happening inside our heads, we simply turn to the other and say, "the crazy story I'm telling myself is…" and then the other gets to reply with what is really happening for them. It has served as a great reality check, opening my mind to just how differently we all see the world, how different each of our "apples" is. *In a curious mind, there are endless possibilities; but once we think we know the truth, our minds shut off, and we focus only on our personal view of the world.* As Bertrand Russel said, "In all affairs it's a healthy thing now and then to hang a question mark on the things you have long taken for granted."

Which brings us right back to consent. Its importance to all of us is reflected in the fact that new legislation in California is being decided, as I write this, that goes along with this rule. The "Yes Means Yes" bill (Senate Bill 967) will require the presence of a "yes" rather than the absence of a "no." This bill is about sexual consent, so it doesn't apply directly to Cuddle Parties. However, the idea behind it, of "yes means yes," speaks to all forms of consent.

"The legislation additionally clarifies that affirmative consent means both parties must be awake, conscious, and not incapacitated from alcohol or drugs – and that past sexual encounters or a romantic relationship do not imply consent. The California bill also, importantly, specifies that "lack of protest or resistance does not mean consent, nor does silence mean consent." ~ Jessica Valenti theguardian.com. More on this at www.beyondcuddleparty.com.

Difficult Conversation Formula

I will now introduce one of those tools that you can't know, at the time you learn it, how it can change your life. With time, it will become so integral to every aspect of who you are, and how you relate, that you will wonder how you ever existed without it.

A year after I met Reid Mihalko, he introduced me to his Difficult Conversation Formula (see Exercise Two below). It is a simple tool, but it was exactly what I needed to give myself permission to talk about the things I held inside. It takes the form of a script that you prepare, following the template in Exercise Two.

Reid shared with me that it's the things that we aren't saying that are killing our relationships. There were so many days he sat with me, my hands shaking, my voice wobbly, tears streaming down my face, as I tried to read from "the script" I had printed out – words I had painstakingly prepared, using his formula; words to reveal yet another painful, fear-ridden part of myself, something I was certain would render me unlovable. I was still so scared of what would happen by saying it - afraid he would leave, terrified that *this* new piece of information would prove I was unworthy of anyone's love. My body remembered what happened when I spoke up as a child - I was seldom listened to and was punished often for daring to speak my own ideas.

Reid sat with me, kissed my throat, and whispered over and over again, "Thank you, thank you, thank you," asking me to please tell him everything. After I finally got the words out, he smiled his heart–bursting grin, and in answer to the question I always asked, "Am I still okay?" He answered, "I love you more."

I eventually realized that, even if every last one of the things that I was afraid of really did happen - as a result of having this difficult conversation - it would still be nothing compared to how many times they were coming true (with even greater intensity) in my mind. Reid says, "If you have the conversation you think is going to end the relationship, and the other person is still there after you're through, that is when your *real* relationship begins."

I use this formula with everyone in my life - family, co-workers, partners - and I encourage my clients to use it with me. I still use it with Reid. It has changed the quality of my life, and given me back so much energy and time that used to be tied up with "what ifs" and with the fear that people couldn't possibly love me if they knew the real me. *Now I share anything that might possibly make them leave,* and if they are still standing there, I know we have just become closer. These real relationships have become commonplace in my world.

Ask, and get a verbal "yes." It's so simple - and yet the truth behind it, the layers within it, and the places you can go with it can last a lifetime.

EXERCISES FOR RULE #3

1. Try "question-storming" instead of brainstorming. Instead of expecting to emerge with an answer, intend to come away with a few new, powerful questions that can take you in a new direction or provide momentum on your current trajectory.

    Rothstein and Santana, of The Right Question Institute, spent nearly a decade coming up with this simple formula:

    A. Design a question focus. (Start with something in your life you are stuck on, such as the belief that a particular action or inaction makes you unlovable.)

    B. Start producing questions and write them down. Change statements into questions. Do not try to debate or answer them (e.g., Instead of "If I say no, Pete won't love me anymore," try "Does saying no preclude Pete from loving me?").

    C. Improve your questions. The ones that require a simple yes or no, make them a little broader. The ones that are too far-reaching, sharpen their focus. E.g., "Is my inability to look Pete in the eyes affecting how he feels about me?" Try instead, "What are the thoughts Pete could be thinking when I'm not able to meet his eyes?"

    D. After question-storming for five to fifteen minutes, prioritize your questions. Pick your top three to move forward.

    E. Take those three questions and begin asking "Why?" (frame the challenge and learn more about it), "What if?" (generate ideas for possible improvements), and "How to" (build on your ideas by going to work on those possibilities).

2. Use the script below, created by Reid Mihalko, to begin saying the things you have been putting off. Try having one conversation a week. You can print the script, write your answers in, and read it right off the page! The most important thing about this exercise is that you get to release what's rattling around inside your head (make more space).

Reid's Difficult Conversation Formula in Two Steps

(From **www.reidaboutsex.com**)

Step 1 – Prepping Your Difficult Conversation

Find some time alone and write down the answers to the following questions, in the order they appear. Just write for three to five minutes on each question, non-stop. Try to keep the pen moving or your fingers typing for the full three to five minutes. Write all the crap swirling around in your head and get it on paper or a computer screen. If you get stuck, write: "I'm stuck. I can't think of anything…" until your brain unsticks itself. Keep moving!

- What I'm not saying to ___(my partner, my boss, the hottie at the bar)__ is **A**.

- What I'm afraid might happen if I say it is **B** (Remember, you're brainstorming! Your list can't be too long! The longer the better!)___.

- What I'd like to have happen by saying this is **C** (Write down all the positive things you can think of!)____.

Step 2 – Organizing Your Difficult Conversation

Cut and paste your answers into this script below, which will be the script that you can memorize, or read from, when you talk to the person you intend to communicate with. It can also be the script that you use to email them, etc.:

Dear ___(partner, boss, hottie at the bar)__, there are some things I've not been saying to you. I'm not saying them/haven't been able to say them because I'm afraid the following might happen:

- (Answers from B here)

- (Answers from B here)

- (Answers from B here)

What I would like to have happen by my telling you is:

- (Answers from C here)
- (Answers from C here)
- (Answers from C here)

And what I'm not telling you is (Answer from A here).

Thank you for listening. What, if anything, would you like to share?

An Example

Here's an example of a Difficult Conversation Formula Script all filled in with a situation that, unfortunately, might be all too common these days:

"DEAR PARTNER, THERE ARE SOME THINGS I'VE NOT BEEN SAYING TO YOU. I'M NOT SAYING THEM BECAUSE I'M AFRAID THE FOLLOWING MIGHT HAPPEN:

- YOU WILL LOSE ALL RESPECT FOR ME.
- YOU'LL DIVORCE AND LEAVE ME.
- YOU WILL NEVER FORGIVE ME, AND I'LL HAVE NO CHANCE OF REBUILDING YOUR TRUST IN ME.

WHAT I WOULD LIKE TO HAVE HAPPEN BY MY TELLING YOU IS:

- FOR YOU TO KNOW THAT I WOULD NEVER LIE TO YOU AND THAT YOU TRUST ME MORE
- THAT WHEN I LIE OR HIDE SOMETHING FROM YOU, I'LL TRY TO COME CLEAN AS QUICKLY AS I CAN.
- THAT WE REACH A DEEPER LEVEL OF LOVE, TRUST, AND INTIMACY IN OUR RELATIONSHIP.

AND WHAT I'M NOT TELLING YOU IS I WAS LET GO FROM MY JOB A WEEK AGO, AND I WAS TOO AFRAID AND ASHAMED TO TELL YOU, AND I'VE BEEN SPENDING MY DAYS AT STARBUCKS APPLYING FOR JOBS WITHOUT MUCH SUCCESS YET.

THANK YOU FOR LISTENING. WHAT, IF ANYTHING, WOULD YOU LIKE TO SHARE?"

Rule #4: If You Are a Yes to an Invitation, Say "Yes"; If You Are a No, Say "No"

The dance of yes and no: "When you live an intentional life and make your own decisions, you come to see the paradox of your personal sovereignty. To follow blindly your own desires will create a prison of constant cravings and longing, from which you cannot escape. To refuse your desires creates another kind of prison, one in which you feel ashamed, guilty, resentful, or even psychologically dead. To engage in your desires, with the recognition that they will teach you about your limitations, your vulnerability, and your conflicts, as well as your strengths, will lead to the discovery of your own nature, of who you are. Learning to be guided but not driven by our desires requires that we learn to hold the tension between blindly following impulses and denying the well-spring of wisdom the soul desires. If we can 'engage' desire, we will learn who and what we are." - Polly Young-Eisendrath

Cuddle Party begins this rule very simply: Say "yes" if you're a yes, and "no" if you're a no. But just because something is simple, that doesn't make it easy. In this chapter I am going to break down some of the stories and feelings that may be happening behind the scenes of your coming up with your own clear yes or no, in hopes that this rule will offer you (just as it offered me) a brand new lease on life as you are able to answer from your own voice deep inside - not from society, parents, religion, or what you have been told.

What if your "yes" was the most joyous sound on the planet, both to you and to others in your life? In Cuddle Party, this rule talks about giving ourselves permission to say "yes" when someone comes up and gives us a yummy request. We are asked not to hold back – holding back comes from being afraid we aren't worthy of whatever it is we are being invited to. My upgrade for this rule is the following: What if you didn't have to wait for someone else to ask you something, to make a request, or to offer you an invitation? What if you began allowing yourself to imagine the things you *could* be a yes to, the things you *want* to be a yes to, and then go out and make the invitations yourself?

One of my first examples of this was in high school, when my friends would sit at home Friday night, hoping that Special Someone would call them up and ask them out. Or they would be at a school dance, or at a dance club with me, and the same thing would happen! We would get dressed up, enjoy the flurry of excitement as each of my friends would share who they found most attractive in the room, and then my friends would spend most of the night dancing together, going to the bathroom together, and lamenting that their "crushes" weren't coming to ask them to dance.

Meanwhile, I walk in the room and zero in on the cutest guy there and, just for fun, get my friends to dare me to walk over and be the one who asks.

With the exception of Michael back in 7th grade, and one other guy who had a girlfriend, they said "yes" every time!!! I would offer to ask the other cute guys for my friends and, every once in a while, my friends would be okay with it, but usually they had all these reasons as to why it had to be the guy asking. To this day, I am so happy that I did not miss out on one of those dances, or those Friday night "dates" because, in that way, I was able to ask for what I wanted.

There is such beauty in getting to know yourself well enough to get to your yes; to be able to dare yourself to ask for those things! Even if everyone was a no to your requests, each time you asked, you are giving *yourself* a HUGE yes!

This rule is also about reducing our own discomfort with saying "no" to people. Many times in life, in order to help ease another's feelings, we camouflage our no, or make a joke out of it. We often act as though we hope another person won't notice when we are saying no, and yet at the same time, hope that they will somehow miraculously abide by our no anyway.

Cuddle Party offers great ways of recontextualizing what no means. A no is really just a yes to something else, usually to yourself. Imagine that you have drawn a bubble bath, that you have your favorite music playing in the background, have candles and rose petals in strategic places, and are about to undress, when you hear a knock at the door. You find it's your best friend inviting you out to a concert you have always wanted to see. You have a choice in that moment: do you say yes to your friend and the concert, thus saying no to you and the alone-time you had planned, or do you say no to your friend, which is just a yes to you?

As you begin answering no and hearing no from this place, it goes right back into the reality that there is no such thing as rejection, and a no is a powerful gift.

Your no is also useful information! Just as you would not feel bad telling someone they needed to make a U-turn if you knew they were traveling in the wrong direction (i.e., away from their destination), it's the same thing with your no at a Cuddle Party - and in life generally. Your no is useful information for the questioner to navigate with. Your no leaves them free to keep asking until they find someone who is a yes, and it leaves you free to continue as you were.

Another key point about this rule is that even if another is disappointed by your no, they will be just fine! When you can begin to allow the people around you to take care of themselves, it is such an amazing gift to them. Stop enabling them by trying not to hurt them, by trying to protect them, by trying to mind-read what they need; just stop. People want to be able to feel their feelings fully. When you can stop making their feelings mean anything about you, it becomes infinitely easier for you to just be with them as they feel whatever they are going through.

We often have emotions come up that, for whatever reason, we think are inappropriate to feel – so we stuff them down. They then settle and become stuck in various parts of our bodies. So when you are lucky enough to encounter a person who allows you to just feel what you are feeling, or a container such as Cuddle Party, which is set up for all emotions to be welcome, it is a gift to allow yourself to experience just that.

Let's use this as a springboard into the next part of this chapter.

I was invested in not making other people uncomfortable. I had a hard time saying no, and I continuously made another's no mean that I wasn't good enough. One of the greatest days of my life was the day I learned that another's no actually set me free.

Ironically, this "no" story has Reid in it; Reid, who has been the key to so many "yeses" in my life. On this particular day, I had sent an invitation to Reid to teach with me at an event. A teaching gig with Reid is one of my most treasured occasions, and I made my invitation as enticing as possible. But something happened when Reid and I finally got to discussing what I was planning.

Reid could do the event – that was clear to me. And I knew that, because of the joy he takes in teaching with me, and our close dynamic, I could probably sway him to say "yes." But, for the first time, I could sense that his saying "no" would be better for him, because it would allow him to rest and recharge.

This was the first time that a "no" did not feel as though it meant anything about me. I could be so proud and happy for Reid, taking care of himself – and at the same time, I could mourn and be disappointed about this particular event at which I would not be able to work with him.

He said "no," and I answered with the following words: "Thank you for taking care of yourself." I had pronounced this phrase hundreds of times – at Cuddle Parties, and in response to people's personal nos. But I had never totally meant those words, until that moment.

After Reid and I had finished that phone call, I sat down and cried for a long time, allowing myself to feel fully my sorrow for not getting to teach with him at that event - and I also cried tears of great joy; joy because I felt like a part of me had just been freed to be able to offer my own "no" more truly. And because I felt that I could begin asking for more things, now that I was genuinely grateful for another's truthful "no." A transformation began, deep within, from "It is more kind to say yes than to say no," to "It is one of the most kind, caring things you can do - for you, and for another - to speak your most authentic no."

Robert Augustus Masters said it beautifully:

In blind compassion we don't know how to — or won't learn how to — say "no" with any real power, avoiding confrontation at all costs and, as a result, enabling unhealthy patterns to continue. Our "yes" is then anemic and impotent, devoid of the impact it could have if we were also able to access a clear, strong "no" that emanated from our core.

A "no" is like our shutting the window between ourselves and the influence of others. "No" is a moment of clear conscious choice. It announces, with clarity and resolve, that your needs take priority. As an affirmation of self, it implicitly acknowledges personal responsibility. Saying "no" expresses the fact that although each of us interacts with others, and that we love, respect, and value those relationships, we do not and cannot allow ourselves always to be influenced by them. It is about refusing to compromise our own center to please another.

One of the most interesting questions that come up at panels and discussion groups I participate in is, "How do I know if I am really a no, or just being ...?" The word to fill in at the end might be "afraid," "selfish," "lazy," or a myriad of others, but in all cases the core question remains: "Is my 'no' ok?"

For example, if a friend is moving and needs help, and you really don't have anything else going on but you just don't want to - is it okay to say no?

The simple answer is, of course. Obviously, say no if you are a no - just understand that there may be consequences. Your friendship may suffer. That person may be less willing to help you, when you are in need. They may be unwilling to call on you, the next time they need help. But more important than that: you may be offering a "no" in order to avoid dealing with a more important issue. Maybe you don't want them to move, and your no is a subconscious statement of opposition to the move itself. Maybe you were once injured during a move, and now have fears associated with this activity. Maybe other factors are in play that you do not wish to face.

This is a Cuddle Party rule that focuses on *honoring yourself*, whether you are a yes or a no. The next chapter will deal with whether you are a TRUE maybe - so, for now, set that option aside. Here are a few questions to ask yourself, to help decide if you are really a no.

If I say no to this, what am I saying yes to? "No" is a complete sentence, but it does not exist in a vacuum. Not helping your friend who is moving frees you up to say yes to something else, whether it be to study for a big test, to catch up on some much needed "me" time, or to visit with another friend. It is not so much "yes" or "no", it's "this" or "that."

Is my "no" really a conditional "yes"? In Cuddle Party we say, "What if I am a yes to the person but not to the request? Then it's time to negotiate." Let's say I wouldn't really mind helping my friend move, but the thought of having to show up at 6 a.m. fills me with dread. I would be willing to help if I could arrive at 10. With this information, I can offer my friend a conscious choice as to whether they want to change the moving time, or move without me ... or maybe even simply start without me.

As we begin the practice of recalibrating all this within ourselves, building up how powerful, respectful, and kind our no truly is, here are some tools to make it easier. (These are excerpts are from Judith Sills' "The Power of No" from PsychologyToday.com.)

No is both the tool and the barrier by which we establish and maintain the distinct perimeter of the self. No says, "This is who I am; this is what I value; this is what I will and will not do; this is how I will choose to act." We love others, give to others, cooperate with others, and please others, but we are, always and at the core, distinct and separate selves. We need No to carve and support that space. (Go to beyondcuddleparty.com for more on "The Power of No".)

It is so much easier to find your yes, once your no has prepared the way for it! Your no breaks down all that is in the way of finding your deepest yes.

If you are saying a hundred no's in the service of a single yes, then each no becomes a part of that yes: they pave the way for your bigger yes to come to the forefront.

Every yes you utter implies a thousand no's you did not choose.

So long as your no remains in service to your ever deepening trust in your ability to say yes, it is one of the most powerful gifts you can offer yourself or anyone close to you: for a person who cannot say no, their yes has no meaning.

Your no has certain qualities that yes just does not possess. A "no" is just "yes" to you! There seems to be a common myth in "new age" circles that, to be a loving person, you must eradicate the use of "no" - the belief seems to be that, in order to show unconditional love, you have to accept everything; that to demonstrate enlightened non-attachment, you must be willing to tolerate anything.

But there's a vast difference between judgment/discrimination, and discernment. Have you ever noticed times when there is a "no" almost screaming from within you? A "No! That does not sit right with me!" Often it occurs when you cannot state a good, strong reason, and don't know why you want to say "no." It's just a "no" that burns in your heart like a bonfire. You used to be able to ignore these promptings of your truth, you used to stuff them down. I hope you cannot do that anymore! I hope that you can no longer hide from yourself. What a gift! For if you dare to embrace an urgent "no", it will provide you with a foolproof roadmap, with knowledge of the truth of anything and everything for you.

It gives you an immediate "Yes" or "No" where a choice can be made. In living from your heart, you are in direct communion with your own "Truth Teller." You will notice that there are a lot of "no's" being given to you at any moment. So, are you listening? Are you courageous enough to stand in *your* "no" where previously you would have doubted yourself, and been often swayed by another's apparently powerful and persuasive "truth"?

Your inner truth teller is always saying "yes" to your being all you can be, even in the "no's" that come. It is guiding you to stand tall in your own knowing, to not be fooled by past beliefs or by old habits of giving away your power of knowing. Do you want to have less self-doubt? Then listen well to your inner truth teller, and heed your "no" as well as your "yes."

This entire rule is inviting you to be fearless in your asking, and to remember:

Getting a no does not mean you're a loser.

Telling someone no does not make you a heartless monster.

No simply means no. Don't take it personally.

EXERCISES FOR RULE #4

1. This week I challenge you to receive 50 "no's." Because when it's okay for people to say no to you, you are giving them the choice to be able to say "yes." Practice taking away the fear: Take 15 minutes and write up as many bold requests as you can come up with - those things that everything inside of you is a big yes to, but which are super-scary to ask for. Go ask for them!! Get out there and ask away - to friends, lovers, strangers - everybody around you becomes a "volunteer." The person sitting across from you may just say "yes," and you may receive something you would love, but the name of this game is getting "no," so either way you win!

2. Open Youtube, and type in "Cat Stevens (If you want to sing out)." Listen through the song once, and then sing along the second time. Really let the lyrics reach you deep inside: this song captures the essence of this rule so beautifully! It's ALL up to YOU!!

Rule #5: If You Are a Maybe, Say No

The price you may have to pay to live your dream is facing your deepest darkest fear but the reward you receive from this courageous act is the realization that your fear was an illusion and that your dreams were always real. If you want to be happy and really live your dream you have to take a stand and just put yourself out there. You might fail, yes indeed – but, you might, you just might succeed too! Don't you want to find out? Either way your life will never be the same...Can you handle it? ~ Jackson Kiddard

"Freedom means the capability to say yes when yes is needed, to say no when no is needed and sometimes to keep quiet when nothing is needed--to be silent, not to say anything. When all these dimensions are available, there is freedom." ~ Osho

This is my favorite Cuddle Party rule of all! More than all the rest combined, it has been utterly transformational in my life.

It sounds so simple, right? "If you are a maybe, say no," and it is a simple concept, but as you put it into practice, you begin to reveal layers of other gifts that it offers. In this chapter I shall discuss a few of those layers that have been instrumental, on numerous fronts, in helping me reclaim my voice.

In Cuddle Party we use this rule (say no if you are maybe) because so often we say "maybe" or "maybe later" because we are afraid of disappointing the person making the request. The person is likely to wait a little while, and then to diligently check back with you to see if now you are a yes. If you again tell them maybe, this time they wait half as long, and then come back to find out if you are a yes, *now.* You are getting frustrated, wondering why they don't just get a clue, when in actuality they are doing only what you told them to do: you said "maybe later" and it is later, so they are circling around to see if you are, now, a yes.

Their excitement, and their waiting on you for an answer, can feel like pressure. The easiest way to let you both off the hook is to just say "no." That puts closure on their request, leaving them free to ask others - and thus they increase the chance of finding someone who is indeed a "hell yes" right now. Even more importantly, it gives you time to figure out whether you might become a yes if A, B, and C were to happen. As an example, suppose someone made a request for you to cuddle them while they talked about their day with you. Suppose the room happens to be very loud - so, although you would like to do that with them, a part of you is not sure. You realize you are a maybe, so you tell the person making the request, "no." A little while later, you have the idea of making a small cuddle corner, in a quieter part of the room, where you would be able to hear them clearly. You can then approach the person who made the original request, to see if the offer is still on the table. If they say "yes," you offer your modifications, and if they are still a yes, you're a go!

And the greatest gift of all is that you have given yourself time to continue to find out, in your own mind, if you are a no *before* you begin an activity with a person, instead of becoming sure of it when you are already in the middle of it – something to which you said yes, when you were in fact just a maybe. It is a lot more awkward, and almost certainly much more disappointing for the other person, when you say "no" at *that* point than it would have been if you had just said "no" to begin with.

As we begin practicing this concept, one of the first skills we begin developing is greater awareness, and we experience interactions that arise more deeply and surely from the truths our bodies are telling us. Our bodies never lie. To figure out if you are a yes, no, or maybe, the best place to look is inward, noticing the clues your body is sending you - slight sensations, warmth, cool toes, a quicker heartbeat, holding your breath, mental fog, gut reaction ... the list goes on and on. If it feels "good" you are probably a yes; if it feels unpleasant, you are probably a no; and if the signals are confusing, it's probably a maybe - which, for now, treat as a no.

My most profound experience of this principle happened when I was ten years old. The most popular girl at school was having a slumber party for her birthday. My family moved from house to house so often that I never managed to get invited to the popular hangouts but, for whatever reason, this girl invited *me!* From the moment the invitation was given, two things happened almost simultaneously: a part of me felt queasy, apprehensive that going to the party would not be in my best interest: I was nervous about mixing with the popular girls, and I feared that I might be better off avoiding a party where I might make a laughable impression that would haunt the rest of my time at that school, but another part of me, the super-stubborn side of me, buckled down for the long haul; whatever it took, I was going to that party.

My family, being very religious, resolved everything by prayer. My mom asked me to go pray about it, and if I had a good feeling, she would let me go, but she wanted me to take my eight-year-old sister as well. When I prayed about going, I had all sorts of alarm systems going off inside my body: my mouth was dry, a major headache was developing, and my tummy felt even worse. It all intensified because, as I knelt in prayer, I knew that in order to go to the party, I would have to do something I almost never tried, something I usually couldn't do even when I wanted to: I would have to succeed in telling a lie, in this case a lie about feeling good about the party.

I practiced in front of the mirror, summoning memories of all the times I had felt good, and on everything my imagination could conjure up about how amazing this party would be. Somehow I pulled it off; it was one of only two times I got away with lying to Mom (I tried a few other times, but my non-poker face always gave me away) and so she sent me and my little sister off for a night of our dreams. Oh, it was a dream, for sure - a nightmare!

From the moment we got there, the other girls picked on my sister. They separated us into different rooms, and to me a whole other world was revealed. The parents were upstairs drinking and arguing most of the night, and so were oblivious to how the girls had put on cable TV, with a movie about a serial killer who strangled women in public bathrooms. I had never seen a movie or TV show that would have been past a G rating. (To this day, I am wary of public bathrooms, always watching the tops of the stalls to make sure no wire garrotes are descending on me.) I kept closing my eyes, but the girls would make fun of me, and there was nowhere else to go. I finally "escaped" into sleep but awoke to the girls dipping my fingers in warm water, trying to get me to pee. It was pretty late by then; the girls all wanted to go outside and toilet paper the neighbors' yards and cars. My sister wanted to watch that, so I ventured outside with the rest of the giggling preteens. Ten minutes later, the birthday girl's dad came outside, threatening us all back inside with a rock salt pellet gun. He shot one round into the ground and, needless to say, the cops were called, all the parents were called (including my mom), and I was not allowed another sleepover until I was 15!

It was a valuable lesson, and if I had been following Rule Number 5, the instant I felt conflict come up in my body I would have recognized the signal that I was a maybe, so it would have been a world easier to just say "no" at the beginning than to have had to collide with my deep "no" in the middle of the activity.

The best part about this practice is that, over time, you begin to develop muscle memory (just as you do with working out at the gym on a regular basis) in becoming more aware of your body's responses to requests and invitations, and it becomes ever easier to check in and recognize what your body is telling you. Your yes becomes more fulfilling, your no becomes more powerful, and you get a great sense of what a maybe feels like to you.

The next level of this rule I want to cover is this: once you have developed a strong response of "no" to your own internal maybe, the next step is diving into your "hell yes." In being able to track the things that light you up the most inside, you begin saying "no" to anything that is less. It looks a little like this: Someone asks you to your favorite restaurant; they are interesting enough, but even with the enticing offer of your favorite food, you aren't tingling and ultra-excited for this outing, so you make the choice to say "no" and you use that time doing something that is truly alive for you in that moment. The thing I enjoy the most about this particular upgrade is that when you have lovers, or a community, interacting this way with each other, it takes away that nagging voice that often wonders if the person *really* wants to be doing this thing with you. When that voice of doubt no longer weighs in, you begin to relax, and your connections become less an "investment" and more a celebration, because everyone is opting in with a choice that is the most purely positive. It also leaves everyone free to begin asking for the things they *really* want, instead of the things they think another would be a yes to. It cuts back on your trying to mind-read, because you now trust that the person in front of you will say "yes" only to the things to which they are a "hell yes."

One challenge I have heard people bring to this rule over and over is "What if I am always a maybe? Then, if I followed this rule, I would be saying no to everything!"

My response is that this is a problem only when they think they will be missing out on something, when they fear that perhaps this will be the "only" time this invitation will come around. I was someone who genuinely based the decisions in my life on trying not to miss out. I overstretched, overpromised, and did a lot of things but none of them really well. I spent 40 years of my life trying to do everything, only to discover a simple truth - are you ready to hear what I discovered?

It is that the only way you *can* ever miss out is in *fearing that you might* miss out.

I want to emphasize the underlying principle here. When you spend all your time and attention trying to accomplish everything, your focus is always a few steps ahead of you, or trapped in memories of "should haves." Either way, your focus is not *with you*, is not celebrating fully in the "hell yes" of this moment, is not celebrating the thing you did decide to do, the person you are with, and the activity you are currently involved in. Again, so simple, but rarely easy: it takes time to retrain yourself to trust that you are listening internally and, with that as your basis, to thus be able to trust that where you "should" be *is* exactly where you are.

A man, who had come to Cuddle Parties for three years, occasionally ventured into the cuddle mosh pit to ask if he could massage or hug someone. Then one Cuddle Party, out of the blue, I watched him go up and ask someone if they would be willing to give him a massage. He was stammering, and looked absolutely mortified, but this woman gave him the biggest smile, and actually responded "Hell yes! I would love to offer you that; thank you so much for asking." This gentleman lit up; he relaxed into her touch, knowing there was nowhere else she would rather be. They exchanged bold requests for the rest of that Cuddle Party, and in all his subsequent parties I have seen him asking for his own hell yeses with confidence and assurance, honoring a no when it arrives, and dancing in celebration when a "hell yes" matches his own.

As was said in one of my most popular Facebook statuses ever, "No more guesses; just no's and hell yeses."

This brings us to an additional upgrade: This is the only time I will be using the "F word" in this book. I hope that what I am writing will be used as a tool for young adults as they are practicing using their voices, developing their own boundaries, and stepping into confidence around being themselves with everyone they meet. Mark Manson wrote an article that takes everything we have been talking about even a few steps further.

> *The Law of "F--- Yes or No" implies that both parties must be enthusiastic about the prospect of one another's company. Why?*
>
> *Because attractive, non-needy, high-self-worth people don't have time for people who they are not excited to be with and who are not excited to be with them. This is the ultimate dating advice lesson — man, woman, gay, straight, trans, furry, whatever — the only real dating advice is self-improvement...*

I encourage you to read the whole article, which can be found at **www.beyondcuddleparty.com**, but I warn you if you are offended by cussing, you may want to skip this one. The point is made powerfully and passionately and with prodigious use of the F-word.

Two profound precepts emerged from adopting this ideal. The first is that even though I practice this rule in so many ways, often on a daily basis, it still can be difficult. Sometimes unbearably so. I wanted to add this part in for the days you may curse my name for introducing you to this concept. There is so much for you to uncover about yourself when you begin to explore the intricacies available to you as you continue to distinguish between your own yes, no, and maybe. Then the "difficulty" doesn't have to preclude fun, as you start to recognize the changes and shifts in all of your relationships, beginning with yourself.

Secondly, I am going to ask you to put aside a belief that we have all been handed since childhood. (You can always pick it back up again when you finish this chapter.) That is the idea that selflessness, and being of service, are "good" and that self-centeredness and greed are "bad." What if you could reclaim self-centeredness as "centered in self" or as a beloved? Shawn Roop says that it is a call to return home.

I'll share a vulnerable example that began 5 years ago. I had been traveling back and forth from Utah to San Diego (a 7-hour drive) once a month for almost 3 years. I desperately wanted my husband and three sons to be a part of my ever-growing community and chosen family in Southern California. So when they started talking about moving out there, I couldn't wait. We moved within 3 months. We sold or gave away everything that did not fit in the back of a truck, and all five of us moved into a friend's one-bedroom RV.

For me, things went well. I was in my element, and I had my family and my community. I was living the lifestyle that I had only tasted up until that point. My husband and oldest son looked for work, my two younger sons did their best to fit in with a culture that was totally different from the one in which they had grown up. They tried really hard but eventually began just going through the motions. They each became more despondent, and we all became more distant. Because at "home" it felt so miserable, I went from traveling and teaching abroad once every few months to saying yes to more and more events out of town.

My oldest son was the first one to return to his center; he rented a car, packed his few belongings, and headed back to Utah, there to start anew. It was a full year later before the rest of us threw in the towel.

We had a clearing conversation, with many tears, a few raised voices, and a lot of regrets: me for not having realized the extent to which California wasn't working for the rest of my family, they were there only for me. They each had regrets: for not having spoken up sooner; for their desire to take care of me and make me happy, which overrode their own desire; and for their eventual need to move back to Utah. Even after we had these realizations, there weren't any easy answers. I didn't want to leave San Diego. My husband had over-given, and had stayed in martyr mode for so long that he didn't have any idea where "home" was for him, or how even to begin returning to his center. Our boys moved back with my mom. My husband eventually moved back to Utah too, after he had reclaimed his right to follow his own needs. He retrained himself to be "greedy" so that when he offered service it was a place of abundance and not from a place of "that is what you have to do." A few months ago, I too moved back home to Utah, realizing I could visit all the places that called to me, but that the most "greedy" place I could imagine for me is being a mom. We are slowly retraining one another to each interact from our own truth, our own "hell yes," our deepest center, in order to allow the others to take care of themselves. We are remembering that the kindest, most "selfless" loving/altruistic gift we can offer is the gift of never abandoning ourselves to try and serve another person, ever again!

It can be so easy to fall into what we have been taught: to be loyal, to compromise and meet another where they need to be met, to endure to the end, to receive our reward. But what I want to offer you, with the upgrade of this rule, is that you can have your reward every day, every single minute, and that the joy that you experience - from living life so fully and so filled with energy, and from your needs and values being constantly recognized and met, by *you* - leaves you overflowing with the desire ***to give from your abundance because it's all you've become.*** Life transforms, and you begin to be a role model of permission for others to be "greedy" too, and soon there isn't even a question of "selfish" versus "selfless"; there is just you and me and the joy that is us.

There are so many more subtle layers and context to this rule, I could write an entire book on ones I have discovered and am still discovering to this day. You redirect your energy and focus to diving deeply into your inner landscape when you give yourself permission to "be greedy" and acknowledge the ways that a request could be made even better by allowing yourself to imagine what *could* feel even better, finding ways to give yourself permission to open to even more pleasure and to being clearer on what does and doesn't work for you, and letting go of the idea that you ever could take care of another person's feelings. It is there that you will find joy beyond measure, and find activities and interactions that delight you beyond anything you have previously known or imagined.

EXERCISES FOR RULE #5

1. Go on a shopping trip. You get to pick out the freshest ingredients for your favorite meal. I also want you to pick out one thing that absolutely disgusts you, something you have tried and know you don't want any part of. Finally, you get to choose something you have never tried before, so you have no idea if you will like it.

    a. Next, take everything home, turn on your favorite music, and begin making the dish you adore. Take time to enjoy every step, every sensation, every smell, everything that brings you closer to the moment when you will get to taste it (at which time you let it explode on every taste bud in your mouth).

    b. When it's finished, serve it up on your favorite dish, so it couldn't possibly be any more enticing (That is your "hell yes").

    c. Place the food you abhor on your ugliest dish, and place it in a different corner of the kitchen (That is your no).

    d. Finally, lay out the food that you have never tried before; put it in a totally different corner of the room (That is your maybe).

    e. Now take turns standing in front of each dish, taking it in with your eyes first, then closing your eyes and letting your other senses take over; each sensation becomes a clue for you as to how *your* body responds to hell yes, no, and maybe. The next time you are faced with a difficult decision, close your eyes, feel back to this day, and let your body lead you in the direction of what is true for you in that moment.

2. Take a moment and become clear on something you want – something so good, so decadent, so delectable that you could not possibly deserve that. It could be sex with a supermodel. It might be appreciation and respect from the person you admire the most. It might be a raise that's 20% rather than 2%. It might be

a vacation to that tropical exotic island you have always dreamed of. What is it that you are afraid to want? Are you clear on it yet? Now ask that supermodel, your hero, or your boss. Ask in a way in which you are neither expecting a yes nor certain that it will be a no. Ask in such a way that asking the question is an end in itself and so that, regardless of the response you receive, you have still won.

Rule #6: You are Encouraged To Change Your Mind

Exploring what really is the deal with our thoughts and actions can create a deep freedom. It is not about judgment, it's more about dropping the autopilot actions that are just outdated, tired old strategies from the past. Being fresh with choice is the simplest form of solid freedom you can offer yourself right now. This is called being in responsibility (the ability to respond to life with choice.) PS: It's totally free and you don't need anyone else. - Shawn Roop

"The quest for certainty blocks the search for meaning. Uncertainty is the very condition to impel man to unfold his powers." - Erich Fromm

"Faith means living with uncertainty – feeling your way through life, letting your heart guide you like a lantern in the dark." - Dan Millman

Rule 6 begins with the question, "Anyone ever get in trouble for changing their mind?" How often in your life has someone tried to hold you to something you said "yes" to? How often have you held yourself to a commitment - out of honor, loyalty, obligation, or fear of the consequences if you did not follow through?

When you look closely, it is notable that this rule, all by itself, has the potential to transform your life. Imagine you are out on a date with someone, halfway through dinner, and you realize the date is not going well at all, and that you are no longer a yes to being there. How many of you would have the courage to lay your fork down, look across the table at your date and say, "This really isn't going well. Thank you for the invitation, and the time together; now I'm going home," and then get up from the table and do exactly that? I imagine most of you, definitely the me of a few years ago, would have pasted on a fake smile and gritted my teeth through dinner, biding my time, being polite and staying on the date for "a decent interval," and at last saying goodbye at the door, not letting on that I never would be calling or picking up their future calls. What I have realized through countless practices of this rule is that the kinder thing to do is to change my mind and communicate that change, which frees both me and the other person to do something else that each of us are *now* a yes to, instead of the pre-negotiated, pre-decided action.

Cuddle Party is a place where a lot of our conditioning begins to change; it's a beautiful container wherein it's okay to say no or yes and then change your mind five minutes or even five seconds later. There is no signing a contract when you say "yes," nor does it mean you are necessarily a no forever if you do have enough courage to say "no."

There are several things I love about this rule. The first is how deeply it encourages us to be mindful, to be aware, to be present with whatever is happening right now. As I was writing this book, I got the greatest example of this I could possibly ever share with you. I was in Oakland, going out for a morning of ecstatic dance with a new friend, Peter Petersen. We parked a few blocks away from the event, and walked in the rain to go dance for an hour. It was a really beautiful hour, deep conversation, the beginning of a deep soul connection, and then even deeper movement, with music that touched me at every level.

When we got back to the car, we found the passenger door was unlocked. We both remembered locking it, so we immediately began checking on our possessions. I discovered right away that someone had sought out and stolen my laptop from where I had hidden it in the back seat. I was in shock, since not only did my laptop contain this chapter, and the previous five chapters, of this book, but it and my laptop bag basically carried the last two years of my life. Pictures, hand-written notes of future projects, poetry, The Cuddle Party Rules I had printed and carried with me for the past five years, a flash drive with a video I had been waiting to release, and so much more.

Peter grew quiet, introspective afraid that the horror of losing my computer with him, from his car, would negate the beautiful day and conversation we had just shared. It was so easy to comfort and reassure him: that we were okay, that this was just a minor blip, no one's fault, and there were sure to be gifts to be had from this experience. He stopped worrying, smiled at me, and drove me to the place where I was scheduled to be co-leading an event in the next hour. What wasn't easy was to let my own guard down, to allow Peter, or a myriad of others, to comfort me, to hold me in my grief, allow myself to feel the many waves of feelings threatening to smash me like a tidal wave. I have been "the strong one" for as long as I remember, and I can push through any traumatic event or crisis: it is something I pride myself on.

But this time I broke down. Maybe it hurt too much to hold back, or maybe I was finally ready to see the people around me through a softer lens. Or maybe the lessons I had been offering everyone around me for the past few years, lessons of learning how to receive had finally sunk in, within me. For whatever reasons, I broke down; I asked my co-facilitator if he felt comfortable leading the class on his own, and he said yes. So for the next 3 hours I practiced this rule as deeply as I have ever practiced anything in my life. I allowed myself to just be with whatever was arising, constantly giving me permission to change my mind. Peter and a couple of other friends went with me back to the scene of the crime, to look in dumpsters and garbage cans, hoping to find my case or at least all the papers it had contained, to find a police station to make a report, to search for local pawn shops (all were closed on that Sunday afternoon) to do "anything" to feel like I had some control over the situation.

After a few hours of looking, we gave up. The class I was to have been teaching was still going on in the residence I was staying at, so my friends drove me there and asked me to check in with them later. I went to the building's public laundry room, sat on the washer, and sobbed for the next hour.

Reid Mihalko, with whom I had co-led an amazing event just the night before, answered an earlier text of mine to let me know he was close by. I had taken great pride in all of the ways I had been able to support, and to give back, to this man, who had given me so much, but now all I wanted was to crawl into his arms, to let his broad shoulders and big beautiful heart cradle me. I began to write a message to him, saying this – to let him know I was down the hallway in the laundry room, but over and over I stopped myself from sending it, not wanting to be a burden to him. Meanwhile another beloved, hundreds of miles away, texted me, "I'm sorry" … just those two words, and I immediately wrote back words of comfort for him, and that I would be okay: that "This too shall pass." His answer – that he knew that I knew all this, and that it did not negate his grief – melted me.

I did not think I would ever stop sobbing. To him I poured out my grief and all the processes chattering in my head - and my friend heard me, held me from afar thanked me for sharing. At the end of that conversation I, finally, had the nerve to press SEND on that original, vulnerable text to Reid: a few minutes later, he came hurrying down the hallway. He held me, heard me, and witnessed me as my snotty, red-faced, sobbing, messy self, and he just loved me all the more for it.

Within, I was finding a degree of softness, of receptivity, of willingness to just be held, that I had never permitted myself before. Reid eventually went back to his apartment, off to do his many Reid things, but I was forever changed. For the rest of that day, and for the weeks that followed, I simply rode the waves: of sadness for my loss, of gratitude for the amazing people and events happening in my life all the time, and gratitude for that opening, that softening that has continued into every relationship and aspect of my life - for, and with, my lovers, sons and family, friends, workshop attendees and clients.

I stopped trying to hold up the world. I stopped trying to make everything okay for everybody. I stopped trying to reckon how much might be okay for me to claim and take for myself, stopped measuring this against whether I had given at least that much in return.

In this state of radical acceptance I have found the true playground of the ability to change your mind at any moment, and it is amazing!

Without a doubt, the grandest gift I received from that day, was in feeling everything, appreciating the truth, that everything is here to help us, I softened, I got to spend the next three days in a softened, broken open state, that allowed Peter into my heart, and eventually my life, in ways that had taken other beloveds years to access. When we are willing to interrupt any pattern, hold ourselves compassionately, honestly, we are available to hold everyone/anyone else in our life from that place too. It is the greatest kindness I know that exists.

In many situations in our lives, changing your mind is looked down upon. Parents, teachers, partners, friends, and especially family members drill into us the importance of honoring our word, keeping our commitments, and following through on what we have said we would do or not do.

What if you could be free of all of that? *Even if it's only to practice what it feels like, during the few hours you are in a Cuddle Party container, where not only is it not rude to change your mind, it's actually encouraged.* That is what I experienced as I played with making outlandish requests, answered yes or no to another's outlandish request, and then really gave myself the opportunity to change my mind two, three, fifteen times if I felt like it. There began a fundamental re-wiring of the places in my mind that used to insist that I "get it right the first time." That used to insist that, once saying yes, I needed to stay there, honoring a request for a certain amount of time – which, in turn, had fed into the story that another person's feelings were *my* responsibility.

Throughout the years of attending Cuddle Parties, I began to define what was "appropriate" or "inappropriate" for me, I really began to reclaim these labels for myself, instead of just going along with society's specifications for them. I began feeling comfortable with, and even looking forward to, the awkward moments where I did not know if a request would work the way I was envisioning.

I dared to ask, and if the person was a yes, it was so much fun to figure it out together!

And then the most important lesson of all: I learned that I absolutely did not want anyone doing anything with me for a second longer than they wanted to be there. I did not want people acting out of guilt, loyalty, responsibility - or the Big One: obligation. Even if I really wanted to be with someone in a very specific way, if they were a "no" I could be with *those* feelings of disappointment much more easily, than with the thoughts and feelings that would creep in if I doubted their "yes."

There were a lot of hard conversations with the people closest to me.

I had the opportunity to share my shame around wanting connection: shame about the times when - wanting to do something with them so much - I had bought into their half-yes, their obligation-yes, their desire-to-please-me yes.

I now wanted to step out of that, and into a new way of relating. From each of them, I obtained permission to ask them as many times as I felt the doubt creep in. To ask repeatedly, to check in during a request, to verify that they really wanted to be doing this "thing" with me – and if they *still* wanted to be doing it with me? Eventually this turned into a game, in which each of us tuned into our own bodies to find our yes or no of any particular moment. If we were still a yes, we continued doing what we were doing, be it snuggling by the beach, having a work day together, or engaged in sexual activity – especially the latter.

Then we began to ask one another, what would make it even better? What if you could be as selfish as you want to be, and could ask for anything you want, trusting the other to respond with their deepest authentic answer? Those exercises and experiences were such game-changers, peak experiences, and magical memories that I will always cherish.

This line of questioning led to an even deeper line of inquiry: What if we had never been taught that some things were "appropriate" or others were "inappropriate", "good" or "bad", "right" or "wrong"?

I am going to ask all of you to take another leap with me, to set aside any beliefs you have, right now, on this subject, and to be open, and curious about what I am about to say.

I have often asked this question in class: *If we were never taught the concept, would there be such a thing as inappropriate?*

About three-quarters of the class answers "yes," citing violence around the world - especially violence against children - as evidence for their case.

Having heard the answers, I pause. I ask everyone to take a breath, and then I offer the example of Nature. There are animals who will maim or rape one another, even eat their own young. Through our social filters it could appear very wrong, but in their life it is just something that they do. This doesn't mean that that there are not consequences for our choice of action. F. W. Boreham summarized it well: "*We make our decisions, and then our decisions turn around and make us.*"

On a beautiful, sunny day in Southern California, I and two of my favorite progressive thinkers and co-facilitators were spending time off together at Disneyland. All three of us are in open relationships. We love having deep, vulnerable conversations, and we enjoy touch.

As we walked around the park, and especially when we were waiting in line, we would snuggle close to each other. Our hands entwined, random kisses were given, and we came up with some really juicy subjects to discuss - about diversity, accountability, sex, consent, abuse, shame, money, ecstasy … all of this hardly surprising, since we share a lot of the same frameworks and passions about the world and one's own role in all of it.

As you might guess, there were many raised eyebrows. Other people responded by pretending we did not exist, and my two companions even remarked a few times, "I wonder if we are being appropriate." By the third time, I began randomly grabbing both of their asses (with their permission) just to rebel against any idea of someone's imposing their values on me.

Eventually, that afternoon, I paused for a few moments, long enough to pose the question – "Are there absolutes, in regard to appropriate and inappropriate?" - to my Facebook audience. There were a few answers that were in agreement with me, but the majority seemed to feel that there is an actual, across-the-board consensus as to what is okay, "appropriate," and what is not okay, "inappropriate."

When you can lay down the beliefs we have been handed, and simply go back to Rule Number 6, "You are encouraged to change your mind," and bring it into this context, you have all the space in the world to make decisions and to act as you choose, because you have created the opportunity to try as many do-over's and different paths as you want. Breathe, and imagine just for a moment that you *are* the cause of your own world.

That if you truly believe that you have absolute choice in every moment (including choosing that you will accept the natural consequences of those choices) then there is no such thing as falling into victimhood or martyrdom.

Nothing is *happening to* you at all.

As you drop "have to" from your vocabulary, life becomes a "get to".

It's radical, I know, and there are many different layers and gifts from every rule, so again I invite you to experiment and try what calls to you, and throw the rest out.

There is another gift of this rule. Consider all the ideas of black and white, good or evil, this or that – ideas that bring us into a place of binaries, polarities, opposites. Ready to stretch your mind a little more?

One of my deepest beloveds, Lawrence Lanoff, has an entire workshop designed around this concept. He introduces us to the question: What if the opposite of pleasure is … not what we think? What if the opposite of pleasure is *even more pleasure?* What if the opposite of open is even more open, the opposite of happy is even more happy, the opposite of money is even more money – on and on?

If you are still holding onto the idea that the opposite of pleasure is (fill in the blank), it is because part of you is fighting to hold onto the pleasure you are feeling, afraid to let it go, unwilling to face what comes next. But when you are able to see the opposite of pleasure as even more pleasure, you are not afraid of what is to come – in fact you are looking forward to it! You are open to receiving and expanding the range of your experience. You are free.

What Lawrence is suggesting is a paradigm shift, that of allowing for the possibility that, as you gain a new reference point for pleasure, you have a new experience. As you breathe in, and make space for feeling a new level of good inside your body, try being open to this as being your *new* "normal" – because you are open to the opposite of it as being *even more.*

Once again, as you then experience even more pleasure, breathe it in, become open to the possibility of *even more* than that, your body will reset again to the new feeling good as your evolved "normal" – which can happen over, and over, and over again, as long as you can let go of the idea of this or that – or of anything you have accepted, up to this point – about *opposites*.

If you can drop the idea of having to hold back the opposite effect, you can then relax and begin to experience what you are actually experiencing. If any part of what you just read is calling to your soul, try it out – just for a day, a week if you are really brave. If you don't love how you feel, you can always change your mind and go back to what you did before.

Which brings us right back to what changing your mind is really about: It is responding to the present as the present is – instead of how it was, or how you thought it might be. **When responding to the present – change is normal.**

The past, whether a minute ago, a year ago, or ten years ago, is already over and done.

The future, even the future of three minutes from now, has not yet happened.

If you are always waiting for something to happen (your ship to come in; that special person; the right moment to ask, or say how you feel; things to get easier) then, even if that thing does happen, you will shoot right past it, and just start waiting for the *next* thing on your list of what it takes to be happy, successful, etc.

You have never learned how to relax and to enjoy the Now. Now is right now, this present moment. A moment that evaporates into the past as soon as you attempt to study it. You cannot hold the present: it is beyond our grasp. You cannot keep that perfect moment from slipping into the past. You cannot keep the future from funneling in to your present moment.

Imagine you are driving down the freeway.

The past is your rear-view mirror.

The future is the scenery, the rolling hills, the trees and mountains that are beyond the next rise: the area ahead of what you can see.

The present is your viewable area. What exists in this present moment? Are there trees? Are there birds? Is there snow? Or rain? How many anthills exist in your present moment? Are there roses you could stop to smell? But you can't stop. This freeway does not take you through space, it takes you through time. Yet, as you continue down the freeway of time, you can see the scenery. As you focus your attention on what lies within your present – when you withdraw it from where you have been, and from where you are going - to fully see where you *are*, the colors become richer, deeper; the scents become richer; your thoughts become more grounded; new appreciations arise, concepts become clear. This is Now. Now is a magical place of immense power and possibility that we all too often ignore in favor of what was, or what may be, without really noticing what lies between. The magic of What Is. (Which is always changing). The only constant is change, and change is constant.

In "The Luck Factor" psychologist Richard Wiseman describes a 10-year study on the subject of luck. His conclusion is that there are four principles that lucky people follow consistently - and perhaps subconsciously:

They are skilled at creating and noticing chance opportunities;

They make lucky decisions by listening to their intuition;

They create self-fulfilling prophesies via positive expectations, and

They adopt a resilient attitude that transforms bad luck into good luck.

(From http://www.richardwiseman.com/resources/The_Luck_Factor.pdf)

In summary, lucky people are that way because they pay active attention to the Now. In one case study, he gave participants the task of counting every photograph in a magazine. Those who were historically unlucky tended to take 2 to 3 minutes to count all the photos. Those who had historically been lucky tended to notice the large advertisement on the second page that read "Stop counting, there are 40 photos." Lucky people do not get so lost in the task that they fail to notice the opportunity. They do not get so locked onto reaching point B that they fail to observe, and take advantage of, their surroundings. Awareness is the key.

You can evaluate the past, you can imagine the future, but you can only experience the present. To be truly present with another is a gift, perhaps the most precious and desired of all, even though we do not always realize it. To be here, right here, completely available, that is what we secretly - or sometimes not so secretly - hope other people will offer us, do for us. Think of your best moments with others, weren't you right there, fully attentive, or being listened to? When we are fully in the present, we are offered deep nourishment, energy from the heart, and we have the chance to feel close to another human being.

Another key piece, and deeper realization, that I received from Rule Six, is: We become entrenched in our memories' being a certain way. If we can just change our mind, this leads us to making peace by allowing all of our emotions, and memories, to be fluid and changeable - to color one another, to have the whole spectrum available to them, and for us to see things in all different lights. As I write this book, this last point I want to touch on is one where I am still making discoveries.

When you feel like you have to have a specific emotion all the time - for example, happy – when you give value to that as your top, preferred emotion and are trying always to maintain it or get back to it, you are missing out on the beauty and depth of all of your emotions that make you who you are, that allow you to trust yourself.

As you begin to embrace and honor all your emotions equally, allowing yourself the freedom to "change your mind" and feel something different at any time, you begin to relax and trust that "this too shall pass" - but you also develop an inner surety that whatever you are feeling is beautiful and complete, and that it has a gift for you in this very moment. You drop the need to get back to joy, or ecstasy, or even back in love, when what you are honestly feeling is heartbroken or shattered in this moment.

Recognizing that this, too, is beautiful, just breathe – and allow it to open and soften; allow yourself to trust *you* even more, relaxing into the idea that you are "perfect" exactly as you are. Only then will you find that there is nowhere to go, nothing to fix, change, alter, or adjust: just this, right now - an incredible blend of the hugest emotions you have ever felt.

It is in this space – the place of inviting yourself to be open to changing your mind about anything – that you begin to develop a capacity for quiet inner reflection, and the ability to tune in and trust. You may have never experienced this before. Your own internal "crazy story" voices are settling down, and your emotions seem to be steadying themselves, as your internal thermometer goes from measuring intensities to subtleties.

The greatest change for me came from being open to the idea that, just as I remembered and held onto memories that I had a bad and traumatic childhood, I was now being open to its having been a good, enchanted childhood. That, as much as I have given myself permission to play out all the horrible events I endured when young, I could just as easily concentrate on the magical, enchanted parts instead: it's all a matter of perspective, and it ultimately led to a beautiful and unexpected gift.

I sat down with my Mom, asked her if she would be willing to share stories, memories of my "enchanted childhood."

My mother looked shocked, as though it was the last thing she had ever expected to come out of my mouth. Then … she broke into joyful tears. It was as if, from my having to hold onto the really bad things that had happened to me, she could not give herself permission to acknowledge all the ways she had been a kind, caring person. And, as childhood stories – and stories about other family members who had not been mentioned in years - began to come out, I found I had never felt closer to my mom.

I looked at this beautiful, 61-year-old woman, whose body is getting so tired and worn out, and I realized that there was absolutely nothing I needed to be holding onto from the past – *and,* even more than that, I found I didn't need her to "be the mom I had always wanted," or to be any different from the way she was. I was just grateful for these moments in which my internal stories – and hers - were quiet enough for us both to enjoy relating to each other.

On an even deeper level, I began an inquiry as follows: What if, in my constant desire and flexibility in reaching out to connect to others, when it seemed as though I only ever allowed myself a certain level and capacity of connecting … what if I was just too busy, and the stories too loud in my head, for me to recognize what I needed to *do* to have it? What if it is in the deep place of *letting go of connection,* that the possibility

- of the connection I had sought throughout my life - is *here, now*, and that it always was?

> *While you have, deep within you, a desire for harmonious relationships, there is an even stronger, deeper tenet, or basis of your very Beingness:your desire to be free. And at the basis of your desire to be free is your desire to feel good - and at the basis of your desire to feel good … is an unhindered relationship between you and you. – Abraham Hicks*

One final example of changing your mind involves my own dear husband, who drove the car to take me to my first cuddle party but would not join me. At the time, he did not like being touched: it made him nervous. For the first few years of our marriage he did not even want me to massage him. As I began studying to be a Cuddle Party facilitator, I asked him to help as my assistant: to handle registration, and other duties. He went to a few Cuddle Parties, then a few more, mostly sitting on the sidelines watching strangers interact (who became not so strange, as he continued to greet them and welcome them in, and as he observed that their anxiety mirrored or was even more intense than his own.)

Gradually, he began participating. He began accepting touch, allowing himself to feel it, to learn what it felt like to just relax next to a stranger; to let your guard down and invite them in. He started quieting the voices in his head that told him this was "weird" or "wrong," and he just let himself go into how good it feels to simply share your warmth with another person. He got to where he started a project on Facebook that involved taking a picture of himself and one (or more) other individuals cuddled up (fully clothed) as if they were asleep in one another's arms. It became very popular, and soon everyone wanted to "sleep with" Nathan, as he brought a different, nonsexual context and popularity to an age-old term. It was also an opportunity for him to "touch" people through words. He would post the picture of whom he had "slept with" along with what he saw in them, sometimes after meeting them only that same day. People felt so seen and gratified, and he was able to expand the definition of touch, and to widen his playing ground - and although even now he won't be the first one to go into the middle of a puppy-pile of cuddlers, he will ask for and offer touch in other ways. This has been such a beautiful example for me that Cuddle Party absolutely works, even if you are terrified and actually opposed to cuddling of any sort! It works because in learning you never have to do anything, you are left free to change your mind, to decide you want to.

EXERCISES FOR RULE #6

1. Take a moment and think of 3 to 5 people in your life that you would consider creating a peer group with. Then write an email or a text - or, better yet, call them, and tell them you are reading this amazing book and want to experiment with one of the ideas it suggests. Ask if they be willing to support you in that. The idea is that the 3 to 5 of you would set aside a specific amount of time, each week, to allow each of you, (beginning with you because it's your idea) to get to practice making outlandish requests - or if you prefer, you can make simple requests. The people in your peer group will then take a few moments: breathing, feeling internally, and answering from their core with their most authentic yes or no. If it's no, you can thank them for taking care of themselves; if it's a yes, the idea is that while you are engaged in the activity, any time that doubt creeps into your mind as to whether they really want to be here doing this particular thing with you, you will ask if they still want to be here doing this thing with you. When the predetermined time is up, the next person gets a turn. The second part of this powerful exercise is when they make a request of you – from simple to outrageous - you now get the opportunity to take a breath and to feel into your body to find your most authentic answer to that request. If you are a no, the hope is that they can thank you for taking care of yourself; if you are a yes, then every time your requester takes the opportunity to ask you if you really want to be here doing this with them, it is an opportunity for you to check in with your body, to expand your mind, to drop any "supposed to," and find where your own natural completion happens, to find when you are ready to change your mind and move on.

2. This is a mindfulness exercise, giving you an opportunity to tune into your inner workings and, once finding your own center, being able to offer yourself from that space so as to truly be able to choose who you interact with, and how, and what you experience life as. Find a relaxed position, either sitting or lying down. Once you are comfortable, close your eyes, and place all of your focus on your breath: feel your lungs expand and contract, and place all your attention on your inhalation and your exhalation. After you

have done this for a few minutes - when you feel as if the whole world is comprised of just this breath, then the next - gently open your eyes. Slowly, with a soft gaze, take in each of your surroundings: the colors, the textures, the distance each one is from you. Continue - having some of your focus on your breath, but keeping your attention mostly on simply what you are taking in with your senses in this moment. Once you have, in this way, taken in the room, I invite you to slowly stand, taking mindful steps through the space, with all your attention on each foot as it rises and falls, your lungs' filling with air and then releasing the air. The idea is that you are practicing allowing yourself to just BE in the intangible presence of Now, by means of tangible activities that draw all your awareness to just what and where you are, Right Now.

3. Bonus exercise: Take a piece of paper and draw a line down the center. Next, put "Appropriate" on one side and "Inappropriate" on the other. Take a few minutes to brainstorm, without filter, editing, or judgment, as to what goes under each heading for you. The next part of the exercise is where you begin reclaiming these terms for yourself. I invite you to take one or two items from your list and try doing them, from an objective point of view. Allow yourself full permission to do something "inappropriate" and, instead of holding yourself back or beating yourself up, just feel, open up and tune into your own body. After having done this thing that, in the past, seemed to cross some invisible line, feel into you: does it cross *your* invisible line? Because ultimately that is all that matters. I will caution, here, to do things that do not carry legal consequences: the idea here is "baby steps," to begin redefining where your natural boundaries lie. Ask permission and get consent if you are practicing anything that involves other people. You can also get away with doing "anything" inside your own mind. Let yourself loose: imagine, fantasize, dive deep into those places that others have taught you were not okay, for it is only here you can begin to find where your freedom lies, can give yourself permission to make your own choices, choose your own life, and claim every minute to live as uniquely as you are.

Then do the same thing with a few specific memories. Draw a line down the middle of the page; on the left, put all the negative emotions and "stories," and on the right put all the positive emotions and "stories you have surrounding them. As you begin this practice, you will probably find that you have associated specific emotions with each memory, and that each emotion has considerably more writing on either the left side or right side. The idea of this exercise is to open to the possibility that you could remember the emotion differently: that you can consider a different perspective, and can change your mind about an event that has happened.

Rule #7: Respect Your Relationship Boundaries and Communicate With Your Partner

"He who binds to himself a joy
does the winged life destroy
he who kisses the joy as it flies
lives in eternity's sunrise"
William Blake

Successful relationships are built upon the foundation of bringing committed love to the table every day, communicating your feelings, receiving your partner's feelings and setting healthy boundaries to maintain a sense of independence within the relationship. This allows for love to be given and received, proper adjustments to be made if the line of communication gets fuzzy and still gives each of you the freedom to be yourself and bring forth your unique creative expression. This combination will manifest the strongest and healthiest relationships in your life. And remember, the purpose of relationships is to be happy, to learn and to CO-create a life together.- Jackson Kiddard

When the heart is flooded with love, there is no room in it for fear, for doubt, for hesitation. It is this lack of fear that makes for the dance. When each partner loves so completely that he has forgotten to ask himself whether he is loved in return; when she only knows that she loves and is moving to music, only then are two people able to dance perfectly in time to the same rhythm. - Anne Morrow Lindbergh

I have begun most of the other chapters with how each rule relates to the Cuddle Party framework - so let's shake it up a bit, and begin this chapter with the greatest gift this rule gave me as I began practicing communication, and finding what truly works for me, in the arena of relationship agreements and boundaries.

There is a beautiful way to have relationships. Instead of holding another to the agreements you *think* they *should* have, instead of *making* your lover sign a contract, and give you promises so you can feel better, you get to do a whole lot of self-inquiry, self-discovery, and make agreements with *yourself.*

Keep asking the question, "Who am I?" Allow yourself space to do that each day - to discover it anew, each day. Learn to be comfortable with your own discomfort, with the times you want desperately to control another, to be in control. Those are the times you breathe and ... find a way to let go even further.

When we can love from such an open space, allowing ourselves and our partner room to shift, change, and *be*, then if they continue to choose to love us, the things they are a "hell yes" to become a celebration, not an agreement kept, or a contract obeyed. And the fear that they might leave us changes to a celebration, and to gratitude that they are here *right now!*

I am so passionate about having space to find myself, room to have my experiences, so eager to share my experiences, to speak my most scary thoughts, without my beloved's taking it personally. This is me, and *they* get every right to be them. I love so deeply, I invite *all* of another to show up as completely as they dare. Do I feel fear that they might leave? Yes, that happens – and there are times I desperately wish for them to be a specific way. But *deep deep* down, I want their realness: I value, appreciate, and am so extremely grateful when, even in their fear, they find the ability to sit before me - naked, raw, and showing me those parts that they are most scared of, especially if they know I wish it were some other way.

You, me, each of us, are so brave in that moment, to risk everything, to truly be ourselves - then, and only then, if we are still in "relationship," that is freedom.

Rule Number Seven is all about encouraging open and clear communication. When, in Cuddle Party, I get to this rule, I like to offer, "If you are in a relationship, or even think that you might be, we hope you and your significant other are in consent about your being here."

Here is how Reid helps you determine if you might be in a relationship: If there is someone who heard you say, "I'm not in a relationship" and they would be pissed to hear you say that, then you are probably in some sort of relationship.

It is during my introduction of this rule that I mention that it is advisable for the attendees to have had a conversation with their partner or partners, and to have settled on some basic agreements for this Cuddle Party. I go on to urge everyone there to stick to whatever agreements they have made - for this party. Instead of trying to change them halfway through *this* event, re-negotiate them for the next one.

The example I like to use is this, "Let's say you have agreed to 'no kissing' at this Cuddle Party, but you have had three or four very tempting offers from some delightful lips: please, please, please do not crawl over to your cell phone and say, 'Sweetie, you know how we have this boundary of no kissing? Well, there are a lot of juicy lips here tonight, inviting me to kiss them; I'm going to take that as a sign from the Universe that it's time to change that agreement. Sorry to leave this on your voicemail - bye!'"

Don't do *that*! Instead, take the invitations, and your desire to say "yes" to the invitations, as valuable information, and use it as an opportunity to communicate, to have a deeper conversation with your partner when you get home. Re-negotiate for the next party. Because if there is one thing I *know*, after facilitating over 400 Cuddle Parties and attending over 500 of them, it is that there will always be another one.

(Editor's Note : Some of our readers have questioned this example of kissing, Surmising that kissing should not be allowed at a non-sexual event. Kissing is not necessarily a sexual act. It's all about intention and awareness. When you have the intention to make it sexual, kissing becomes sexual. When you intend for it not to be sexual, it's usually not sexual. If you start off not sexual and get "swept away," when you notice that you've started sexualizing it, just re-commit to your original intention to be non-sexual and it will begin to shift back to non-sexual. This example is used on purpose to get people thinking/talking about this.)

The Cuddle Party arena offers a unique opportunity for people to try out, in real time and in a limited container, things that might overwhelm them in the day-to-day world. Cuddle Parties are a perfect live laboratory, where the attendees know there is a specific beginning, middle, and end. There is someone there – the facilitator - who has their back, as they experiment and expand edges (I talk a lot more about this particular point in the next chapter.)

And they have the option to stop experimenting and leave the "laboratory" at any time. It was so useful for me, as an attendee, to try making new, bold requests, to try on new relationship agreements, or to see how it felt to drop some agreements that I or my partner were asking of each other. Cuddle Party is at most a three-and-a-half-hour experience, so it is much easier to be a yes to trying something new for that limited time, especially the new things that feel the scariest.

People have met and fallen in love at a Cuddle Party, and I know of a few who even went on to get married. I have also witnessed relationships fall apart, as one partner is more eager and excited to explore the freedom of touch and connection offered at a Cuddle Party. They get so excited, and don't think about checking in, before the party, about what their partner is afraid of or hopeful for - or sometimes, even if they have checked in ahead of time, they get wrapped up in the moment and kiss another person, or look a little too long in an intimate eye gaze, in a way that their partner may not ever be open to, and certainly is not ready for in this moment.

I have found that it is usually kinder to play to the comfort levels of the person who is feeling the most challenged, giving them room to trust, to experiment, and to open at their own pace, while at the same time giving each other room to talk about anything, without judgment, blame or shame.

A dear friend of mine, Charlie Glickman, wrote an article that has stuck with me as a highly evolved way of co-creating boundaries that can work in relating with a partner. He is addressing how to talk about sexual interactions, but the same tools and concepts can apply across the board in all relationships. It's titled "I'm not easy. I'm selectively convenient."

I'm not easy. I'm selectively convenient.

(Excerpts reprinted with permission from a blog by Charlie Glickman at charlieglickman.com)

When a friend jokingly told me that I'm easy, I instantly replied, "I'm not easy. I'm selectively convenient." I don't play hard to get, and that doesn't mean that I'm easy.

I have high standards for what I want from a sexual connection, and I have high standards for the people I create those with. I expect people to come to it with an open heart, to be able to tell me their wants, needs, & boundaries, to be able to hear mine in return, and to find a way to have fun within those parameters.

I expect a lot and if I don't get it, I'll start a conversation to see if that will change. If it becomes clear that I won't get what I want and need, or that I'm not offering what the other person needs, I'll disengage with as much grace as possible. On the other hand, once I know that things line up, it all becomes pretty straightforward. That's where the "selectively convenient" piece comes in, because I'll do what I can to make things as smooth as possible. Being selectively convenient is sort of similar to how some dogs and cats operate. They'll check someone out to see if they want their attention. If the answer is yes, they go all in. If the answer is no, they back off. And for some animals, the "yes" list is pretty small, but they don't hold back from the people who are on it. I think "selectively convenient" is a fine thing in any kind of relationship. If you want to figure out what "selectively convenient" means for you, start by thinking about what your selection process is. What are your wants and needs? What are your filters? Can you share them with a partner in such a way that they can hear it and respond? Are you open to their replies? And how will you talk with them to find the overlap between what you each offer and what you each want?

Those conversations take a bit of practice to manage with grace, especially when there aren't a lot of role models for how to do it. Whatever your personal vision of what "selectively convenient" might mean, and whatever path you choose, think about how you're holding yourself back. Then imagine what it would be like if you didn't do that anymore. You'll probably discover that it's a lot easier to get there and the rewards are definitely worth it."

This is such an up-level from when my husband and I got married. We were so young, so inexperienced. I was twenty-one, Nathan was twenty-four. We had so much learning and exploring to do around boundaries.

We had both already had front-row seats at our parents' nasty divorces – and as for me, this was not even my first marriage: I had already gotten divorced from an abusive first husband. One major item we agreed on, Nathan and I: we were committed. Neither of us wanted to put each other, or any children, through the divorce process.

I was a much more social person than he, so - even though I had never been taught what you are reading in these chapters - I attempted to create a few "agreements" to help our union be more sustainable.

The most important one, for me, was for him to accept that I had friends – male and female – with whom I went to movies, others whom I went dancing with, and friends for various other activities. Knowing that Nathan didn't like the majority of those activities, I wanted to make sure he knew that I would rarely ask him to come with me, but that I wanted to keep these friendships as involved as they had been. If that didn't work for him, then perhaps we shouldn't get married.

Let me add, here, that - especially at that time - this felt super scary and risky. I had so much invested, by the time Nathan had finally said "yes" to getting married. You see, I was the one who had opened up first, to our love for each other. What had started as a beautiful friendship, where we were able to talk about and listen to one another's deepest ponderings had, for me, blossomed into such passion, and such a longing to share my life with this person.

Nathan, on the other hand, was still living at home, and was determined to be a bachelor his whole life. He just found dating, and the prospect of marriage, too troublesome – after all, everything he enjoyed was at his fingertips in his own room, his own space. He highly valued autonomy.

I, being Monique, began to propose to him after six months of dating. Sometimes I proposed daily, for the next few months! And one day instead of his usual "I don't think that is a good idea" followed by his reasoning as to why it wasn't a good idea, he said "yes".

His "yes" surprised me, but I didn't let that slow me down, and within a few hours I had my dress, had made an appointment at the local Justice of the Peace, grabbed two witnesses (my ex and my mom) and – as we were sitting in the outer chamber of the court, waiting our turn – that is when I had the courage to bring up the conversation about still wanting the freedom to be me, freedom to interact with people whose company I enjoyed. He sat with my request for a few minutes, and then surprised me with a second "yes" that day. I couldn't have felt closer to another person as I sat there holding his hand, about to embark on a life together.

I could write a whole book on all the openings and transitions that have happened in our marriage over the past 22 years and, perhaps, one day, Nathan and I will write it together. But in this chapter I would like to just touch on a few ways in which we have experimented within the broad spectrum of vows, contracts and agreements.

Twelve years into our marriage, both of us were trying to "do right" by each other, following the limited role models we were able to observe in other couples - following what society, our religion, and close friends said would make a happy marriage. But we were vastly different, and we each had our own issues around guilt and shame - and about worthiness in general: it was like the blind leading the blind. We loved each other so very much and - along with that - deep down we were both exhausted and both pretty miserable. By the time I went to that first Cuddle Party, hosted by Reid in Las Vegas, we were just scared enough to be open to trying things differently.

A few months after that first one, Reid came out to where we lived to facilitate Utah's very first Cuddle Party. We only had thirteen people show up and, for more than half of them, the comfort-level did not go beyond playing Monopoly: they did not even imagine cuddling as being part of the evening. But the greatest gift for Nathan and I was having

Reid stay at our house.

We had a lot of different discussions on relationships and sexuality, the biggest theme being communication. For the very first time in both Nathan's and my life, we had someone willing to listen to our deepest shame, our deepest fantasies, our deepest challenges. Instead of getting lost in them, Reid just smiled and giggled with his unique Reid amusement. We found, through him, that we weren't as different or weird as we thought, as we had always been told. Something began to open inside each of us and, we gave ourselves permission to begin imagining just how a relationship could look, a relationship of our choosing!

For the next seven years, we tried out different agreements, experimenting with what our unique dynamic could look like. We eventually got down to one single boundary, which was that we would agree to have a conversation about anything, the simple principle being that everyone had a right to be heard.

That was our only conscious vow, but the problem was that we had so many unconscious vows running us both behind the scenes. Old habits and patterns that we just fell into, that seemed to make new choices seem almost impossible.

In 2012, we were living in California, and I made the decision to go to Burning Man for the first time. Burning Man is a giant social experiment that is held once a year in the Nevada desert. People come together from all over the world to create a city of truly infinite possibilities. It is off-grid, without phone or internet. The hot, dusty environment pushes everyone to their limits. It was the first time Nathan and I were out of contact for ten straight days. When I got back, we had both come to the separate conclusion that what we were doing wasn't working. He felt like he was always on call for me and the boys, even though we weren't asking that of him, and that he had put his life, his wants, and desires on hold for so long he had no idea who he was any more.

I had never lived alone or relied solely on myself. And our boys had their own ideas: they wanted to move back to Utah, to be with extended family, friends, and familiar surroundings. What we all agreed upon was that my boys would move in with my mom, Nathan would stay in California, alone, to find himself, and I would get on the road full time, to find me. On my 40th birthday, we had an "Unwedding Ceremony."

This is an excerpt, taken from my journal that day…

Nathan Darling, to whom I had been married nineteen years, my best friend and beloved for thirty years and I had decided to take some time apart, to separate, to gift each other and ourselves with the true freedom to find ourselves. We are blessed to have a dear friend who has offered to lead us through a community transition ceremony. My greatest hope in sharing all of this publically, is that it will give our community an opportunity to celebrate this new beginning for us, and on an even broader scale, that it will give a vulnerable journey of an alternative "happy ending" of how couples who love each other very much can live happily ever after. I don't know how any of this is going to look. I went from being a mom to my siblings, to marrying my first husband and having a child at 19, to moving in with Nathan, as best friends, falling in love and being together for 19 years, He went on a mission for the church and then moved directly from his mother's home, where he was very much the father to his siblings to being with me. We are both alternating between deep sadness, excited joyous freedom, and complete withdrawal, wanting to hide from what all of this could mean. Through all of it, we have discovered a place of such deep love that will never ever end.

During the ceremony, we were both held so lovingly, so exquisitely by community and by our two boys who are 12 and 14 years old. We gave each other back our wedding rings with these "unvows".

We have gathered here today to be witnessed as we unbind our two souls from the shackles of societal expectations, from the bondage of unconsciously agreed upon vows, from the oppression of parental hand me down values. To allow the relationship space to grow beyond the confines and definitions that have been handed down from parents, church, society, our own inner voices, to allow it to grow and breathe and open to the truth it can be. To reframe the word "loyal", and our metric of duration of time together, our "conviction" that we had to stay together, to *be* together, and to not fail each other or our children. To recuse ourselves of the role of "crutch" "enabler" "excuse" in hopes of offering the other the freedom to blaze our own trails independently, to be on the same page, without resenting one another, for not being the parent that we ourselves are not. To be able to relate from an objective, safe space. To keep the wisdom and history, and intimate knowledge we have gained over these 19 years of marriage, while releasing the baggage and expectations that have never served us. We offer each other the greatest possible gift, our freedom.

And then community stepped in to hold space as Parents, Society, Church, God, and our children, stood in as Nathan and I consciously asked for each of their blessings to let go of the bonds and vows we had once made to each of them, so that we could begin anew relating from the place we are, the people we are now. It was so beautiful to take back that piece of us that felt we had "broken" our promises, gone back on our own word, to our promises/vows of "for time and all eternity" in our old Mormon faith. To re-center ourselves, to open space for heaven on earth, instead of enduring to the end for our promised reward. There were many tears, many hugs, and so much support!! Ronan (our 14 year old) held out two candles joined at the wick, he lit it, and before the whole community "gave us back to each other," proclaiming "They are the best parents and I love them." As the wick came apart, Nathan and I felt free for the first time in 19 years, free to see one another, to choose anew, in every moment, what/ how relating can look like. I have not seen him as happy as I did last night in a very long time. Thank you friends, lovers, and tribe for being there. I love YOU."

So, do you want to know what happened? After three months, Nathan missed his boys and chose to move and start over where they were at. After a year on the road, I decided the same thing.

You see: When you have every choice in the world open to you, then the actual choice you make is made with such joy. I still travel and teach. Nathan is one of nine lovers I have: we remain married, and it is a marriage of our own making. Being a mom now is one of the greatest gifts ever, because when I could have been anything, mothering my sons is what I choose.

What if ... you are reading this, and being able to communicate and find agreements that work for you sounds intriguing, but seems perhaps a little scary and overwhelming too? Maybe you are wondering where to start. Reid has some simple and useful guidelines for this, in what he refers to as "Dating Your Species." The following is an excerpt taken from his website Reidaboutsex.com:

> *Dating can be daunting when you're looking at so many possibilities. It's wonderful to choose partners based on attraction, but that doesn't guarantee a good match. Ever dated someone you were super attracted to who also drove you nuts?! What if there were a way to upgrade your dating "operating system" and identify the people who would be easy to be in relationship with? Who were your species?*

> *Since relationships aren't about survival anymore, and since you've got more access to people than you did back in "village times," I recommend that you try to scare people away from the start. Be specific in what you're looking for and narrow your "Google search of love." Why? Modern dating is like a Google search: Often, the more specific you are with your search terms, the greater the chance you end up finding what you're looking for. If someone is not a good fit for you relationship-wise, it's better to find out now, rather than when you get attached to them. If you want kids, why date someone who knows they don't want kids ever? If you are polyamorous and would never date someone who isn't poly, lead with that early on. If you're monogamous and aren't okay with your partner seeing other people, don't date someone who's looking for an open relationship.*

> *We often don't want to get specific because we're scared that we'll never find anyone; however, we waste years dating people who are bad fits for us. When you do the math, I think being specific, as a means of weeding people out of your search - while it might take more time and be scarier - yields more happiness over a lifetime. Would you rather be in a series of bad relationships for years on end or be single for a few more years and find someone who's a good fit for you?*

The good news: Putting what you really want out there not only scares the bad fits off, your specificity begins broadcasting to those who are looking for someone like you that you exist!

Figuring out what species you are isn't as difficult as you might think. You've been leaving yourself clues your entire life. Like a CSI television episode, sift through your past relationships for clues as to what worked for you and what didn't. And be honest.

Do relationships work better for you when you date someone who's straight, gay, queer, monogamous, poly, swinger or asexual? Religious, not religious? Has kids? Has no kids? Wants kids? Is close with their family? Has lots of friends? Is extroverted? Is introverted?...

Those might be some of your Win-Wins: Those things that, when present in the relationship/person, make the relationship work SO much better.

Bottom Lines are those things that automatically put an expiration date on the relationship and, if you were really honest with yourself, are not acceptable for you at all. Casual drug use for some isn't a deal breaker. For others, it's a no-go but they "make an exception" because it's "not that big of a deal." But that exception eventually leads to resentment and an inevitable end. Look at your past relationships, especially the ones that crashed and burned horrifically... What actually ended those relationships? Those are probably Bottom Lines for you. Respect what your Bottom Lines are when you discover them and, trust me on this: Do not ever make exceptions on your Bottom Lines.

Wiggle Room... Live in a city or in the country? Likes to leave their socks on the bedroom floor versus keeps the bedroom immaculate? Things that aren't really big deals so long as lots of Win-Wins are present... Welcome to figuring where there is "wiggle room" in your relationships.

Lastly, try to map out those things that don't have to be perfect so long as they're improving. For example, the potential partner isn't great at communication but they love communication workshops and books and courses, and are rapidly improving in this area... That might fall under the 3-Strikes category: Something that, if not addressed and improved, would end the relationship eventually, but you're willing to give space and time for it to shift. The key to 3-Strikes is to actually put a limit on it. If it doesn't improve after a certain amount of time, you must end the relationship.

These four categories are the characteristics Darwin would have used to describe "your species."

Doing the work to discover what your species is and using it to filter out who might be a good fit for you, in love and life, will add immense ease and fun into your relationships and reduce drama. You'll still have things you need to work out - no one is a perfect fit - but a lot of the tension and conflict, that many relationships encounter, evaporates when you're with someone who is your species. Relationships will always be work, from time to time, but that's normal.

When you agree about the fundamental expressions of love and sex, then neither of you are trying to make the other person different. Feelings of being constrained, of being put in the wrong, and being out of alignment all the time can evaporate. (And, hey - if you're already in a relationship with a different species, all is not lost! Sharing and acknowledging the differences and knowing that it's going to take more work can make a big difference, too)." - Reid Mihalko, from Reidaboutsex.com

As I began making my own lists, allowing myself to be as "selfish", shallow, deep, and intense as I chose to be, I found I really had no interest in holding anyone around me to past promises, commitments, and agreements. Instead, I desired to constantly be searching within, finding the ways I could fill myself up, concentrating on keeping my own internal promises and agreements to myself. From that place I came up with my own templates as how to be the most successful in relationship with me.

If you wanna be my lover... you are someone who picks *me* - not every day, but on the days that it really matters. Someone who goes to sleep thinking of me and wakes up delighted that I am in your world, but in the hours between has your own life, your own passions, finding and delighting in yourself. I long for someone who challenges me, who welcomes my challenging you on every level and isn't afraid of me. One who stays centered, no matter what I throw at you. Bonus if you like the occasional psychedelic. and like to wrestle!

Someone so passionate about life, self-discovery, and who you are, that you shine your light all over the world and therefore not only are not afraid of being overshadowed by me, but are excited to be a witness as my light grows brighter too. Someone who wants to touch God through sex, and via everyday experiences, and who wants to explore every shadow side or inner demon that keeps you from being fully expressed. I want someone who truly wants to know me, who truly loves me more for all the parts that we find together and who is willing to grant me access to *all* of your scary parts as well.

I want someone willing to call me on all my shit, who welcomes my calling you on yours. Someone who kindly challenges my beliefs and is honestly curious about the being I am today. Someone who picks me, again and again – and who is ecstatically grateful, and touched, and who opens more because I pick you too. I choose you with all my heart, mind, body, and soul. Someone whose entire being is vulnerable and meets me in the real world, rediscovering each other every day. Someone I can explore my endless passions of sex and spirit with, someone I can call home, while simultaneously we each are our own home. The greatest present of all, to me, is "love" – and how I define it today is the space to meet and be met, gratitude for all that's been, and room for all that can be, while savoring and just being with all that is, with whomever you are with at any given moment.

The key here is that ***it all starts with yourself***, then overflows everywhere else.

Something changes the moment you decide you've found a person you are ready to reveal parts of your soul to. Something stands out and makes the moment unique. As if you do not care whether your heart will melt or crumble in the process because your brief courage undoes your tremendous fear or disbelief. A moment of psychological reward smashing all self-imposed disciplines founded on terror. This is all you need. - Anaïs Nin

EXERCISES FOR RULE #7

Here is one of my favorite workshop exercises. It brings on so much support, and fosters developments that simply cannot be imagined in advance.

Invite two or three people to come share in an experiment with you – partners, friends, colleagues, people you are confident can be cheerleaders for you.

Take a few minutes, each of you visualizing what the world could look like if you were surrounded by your most ideal relationships. Once you have all the specifics, one of you gets two or three minutes to share their idea of a world filled with their version of fearless relating, and then turns around - turns their back to the group. The other two or three people get a few minutes to "gossip" about the person who has their back turned to the group. But this isn't like any gossip you have ever experienced before. In this exercise, you gossip in the following manner. You are all talking as if you have experienced that person's world of ideal relationships. Perhaps you – supposedly - went on a camping trip, or to a party, or simply spent a few days hanging out with them and their ideal family unit, experiencing how awesome and free it was. Talking amongst yourselves, as if the other isn't present.

Taking turns, until everyone in the group has had a turn to be "gossiped" about. Then check in with one another, to see if having others "buy into" your greatest imaginings of relationships has given you more ideas or greater permission to continue creating these in your own life.

Rule #8: Come get the facilitator if there's a concern, problem, or you need assistance with anything today.

True intimacy is the opening of one soul to another. No gift on earth could compare with it, for it touches us more profoundly than our imagination can envision. When two people share their lives, freely, openly, without reservation, it is as if each had become complete. - Robert Sexton

"Until we can receive with an open heart, we're never really giving with an open heart. When we attach judgment to receiving help, we knowingly or unknowingly attach judgment to giving help." - Brené Brown

Gracious acceptance is an art - an art which most never bother to cultivate. We think that we have to learn how to give, but we forget

about accepting things, which can be much harder than giving....
Accepting another person's gift is allowing him to express his feelings for
you. - Alexander McCall Smith

This rule is here to let the room know that there is always a "lifeguard on duty." There is someone who has your back at all times. It gives you the permission and encouragement to explore edges that you might not if you were on your own. From making outrageous requests, to practicing hearing or saying a "no", to perhaps being curious about what it is like to be touched without sexuality's entering into the equation.

For many of the Cuddle Party attendees, just being there, just showing up and walking through the door, is a giant breakthrough. So don't be surprised if it brings up thoughts, feelings, questions, concerns, and exciting epiphanies. The key is to avail yourself of the facilitator so you can share what's going on for you at any time. During the Cuddle Party, the facilitator also participates, so it is important for them to give the audience permission to interrupt whatever they are doing if a participant needs support with anything that happens to be coming up for them – especially if they are feeling confused or distressed, or are having the same thoughts or questions continuously popping up in their head and thus cannot relax into their experience.

It is also another subtle reminder of ways "to take care of oneself." Permission is given, by direct invitation, to come to the facilitator to get help when you are struggling or challenged, instead of your having to endure it or work through it yourself - or sadder still, decide to leave because you don't want to "bring down the group" or "bring that kind of energy" to the party.

One of the greatest take-aways this rule has to offer is that of asking for, and receiving, support. This is all win and no loss. You allow another to be able to be with all your raw, yummy, gooey parts, and to love you more for them. Even more importantly, it gives everyone else in that room permission to open up, to ask for help, and to show their raw, gooey, yummy parts, too! It's an invitation to vulnerability, and "leaning into" support is not only acceptable, but preferable to "manning up" to supposedly show strength by isolating ourselves until our feelings go away. By asking for and accepting a helping hand, we begin to melt away the old paradigm, the old culture of "outwardly perfect while, inside, falling apart," and we see the beauty of vulnerability, and of our ability to unconditionally receive as the new paradigm, the new culture.

As a facilitator, what I offer includes, "If you aren't able to get your mouth to work, raise your hand, and I will come to you - and if anyone else sees a raised hand before I do, tell me about it."

As I attended Cuddle Parties - usually run by Reid - there would come a time during the event, when I would notice he was free, and I would make my way over to him, ask if he would like to cuddle with me, or if I could massage him or walk on his back, play with his ears, all things I knew he liked, and most often, his answer would be, "yes".

After a few gentle prompts from him, coaxing me to share "what was really up," I would ask a scary question or two, make a request - or sometimes just lean into his strong arms, hide my face from the rest of the group, and just cry, each time allowing more of my held-in grief to come to the surface and not have to be held down, so deep inside of me, any longer.

To this day I remember my terror of opening my mouth, of feeling sure that the next few things to come out of it would change how Reid saw me forever. I recall my entire body trembling, as I dared to risk trusting him to hold my requests, my emotions, that everyone else in my life had run away from or punished or shamed me into keeping hidden.

At each Cuddle Party, I thought it would get easier but, if anything, it felt even more scary, like the world really was about to end. Later, I realized: it was because each time I approached Reid, I would open up *more*, take *further* steps in un-hiding my insides and showing them on the outside. And in a way my world *was* ending, after each revealing. It was not possible for me to go back to the way I had been before.

When I began running my own Cuddle Parties, I wanted to "get it right." So, that first year, I would sometimes run six a week! It didn't matter to me if there were three or thirty people; I just wanted to practice holding the space, that had been so masterfully held for me when I had been learning to find my words, find my own internal values, and remember what a beautiful gift it is to just receive.

Do you realize how rare it is to be able to receive gracefully? Giving and receiving are meant to be harmonious dance partners, and it can get pretty clumsy on a dance floor that has one without the other. Most of us are very good at giving: we have been giving for our entire lives. But to be able to fully receive … that is an art. As with any art form, it takes slowing down enough to be able to tap into the dance of surrendering and opening, to the experimenting with a new practice. Time to actually feel it in our bodies, because it is only in the actual experiencing of something that we are able to create new reference points and anchors to return to, to start from, the next time we allow ourselves to go a little deeper, push our edge a little farther, to learn to "take it" (as Reid jokingly puts it), to unconditionally receive what's being so generously offered.

Most of us, as children, received joyously. But as we grow up, receiving tends to be more of a challenge. Feelings of guilt, questions of worthiness, and perhaps issues of reciprocity are likely to have become part of our story. Over the years, many of us have accumulated many "free" gifts that were actually quite expensive when the giver came to collect what was "owed." But it doesn't have to be like that. Cuddle Party is a perfect container to begin practicing how to receive, joyously, again.

Having our gifts received is one of the most pleasurable and nourishing experiences we can experience. If you always say "no" when someone tries to give you something then you're never giving them the chance to feel generous and have that exhilarating experience of giving.

I want my gifts to be received. We all do.

So let's be abundant in our receiving, and generously allow others to feel generous in their giving to us.

True intimacy consists of receiving more and more of the other person. Their gifts, their wounds, their truths. Graciously allowing others to feel received. Because as we receive the gift, we are also receiving the giver.

I love an article I found online by Sharon Warren titled "The Art of Receiving" Here is my favorite excerpt from that article:

Initially, you may feel tender and vulnerable as you open up to graceful receiving. I invite you to actively engage in receiving by taking baby steps. Once you understand the principle of cause and effect, you see how being receptive is part of the magic for the giver. Be willing to receive (without feeling you have to give back). Embrace it. You get to modulate and mold your experience of receiving. Know you are worthy and deserve to receive.

Read more of Sharon's touching article at beyondcuddleparty.com

One of my first beloved spiritual teachers offers another take on receiving:

When you allow you to feel good about yourself by focusing on what you do *so* right that's called the ability to receive.

It is only when you can slow down, stop, and say, "What have I done in my life really well, today?" Give yourself the opportunity to take it in, to feel good about it, to feel good about you, to become a recipient of your own grandest offering. That is receiving! When you learn how to receive, only then will everything you have sought, everything you have learned, anchored, and been creating have a chance to come to you.

The idea is that we are so used to criticizing ourselves, but that when we take the time to compliment ourselves, to really observe and acknowledge all the amazing things we do, it starts opening a beautiful space of receptivity in us. As we practice receiving our own praise, it becomes easier and easier to say yes to what everyone, and even all of existence, has been waiting to gift us with.

I really like that concept of what receiving is.

Another beloved in my life tells of the time he went to see a Tantric Practitioner. His goal was to learn "how to give."

She welcomed him in, and began the session. Within a few minutes, after he had shown her the ways he knew how to give, she stopped him, and said, "You don't need to learn how to give. You give masterfully already. How are you at receiving?"

With these words she touched a nerve. For him, as with many of us, giving comes easily: we get to stay in control, offer what we want, feel like we are adding value, and make others feel good. But to genuinely receive means trusting ourselves so deeply that we can release all control, and just allow another to gift us with what they have to offer; to let go of the voices in our head that are always tallying a mental balance so that we can plan to give back equally.

There is a beauty when you can be just as comfortable giving or receiving - giving for giving's sake, having learned the true value of generosity and how to be a bountiful receiver. It now becomes a delight to offer that which you love to give, without reciprocity's ever even entering into your mind.

As you have more and more experiences of unconditional giving and receiving, you become full, filled up, and have more to offer yourself and everyone around you from that beautifully fulfilled place. *"Giving without expectation leads to receiving without limitation."* - **Charles F. Glassman**

I had been leading Cuddle Parties in San Diego almost every Sunday night for over a year. Typically, half the people showing up would be first-timers and half would be returning attendees - some, on their way to being Cuddle veterans.

On one particular night, it had been a rare rainy day in Southern California, and as people walked in, it seemed as if the rain had broken through many people's floodgates. Even during introductions, a lot of the regulars began to cry, or express disappointment or dissatisfaction about where they were in life. The common theme seemed to be a deep level of loneliness, of despair from the thought, "I will never be met, never be seen or understood."

It was the first time I had experienced "holding a room" with so much emotion and energy happening at once. I took a breath, and invited the group to focus on breath as well, and we allowed extra time - beyond the usual thirty seconds - for each to give their name and why they came to the Cuddle Party that night.

Each person's sharing seemed to open the other people more, seemed to give permission to the next person to be even more vulnerable, and to allow the group to give to them - through compassion, through empathy, and through just a shared sense of their humanity.

There was one particular fellow who had been to many of my events. He would always show up early, and was often the last out the door, offering to give rides to anyone in the vicinity, and usually offering two or three hugs. He was always offering outwards yet, for whatever reason, that night, he really tapped into the deepest depths of his loneliness and desire for a partner. He lay cuddled in my lap, sobbing. In essence, he put a plea out into the Universe, to not have to be alone any longer.

On my left was a lovely lady, who usually came only to those of my events that were just for women. She had, however, felt called to come to this particular coed Cuddle Party. As this beautiful man bared his soul, through tears and a pouring-out of authentic emotions, I could feel her begin to open also. A little while later, she slid closer and asked if she could put a hand on him as well. He agreed and, through a series of mutual reachings-out, questions, requests for deeper connection – all of which were answered with "yes" – they eventually had become a tight little cuddle. She was holding him, and he was leaning into her, not even pretending that he had anything to give – for those moments, so utterly receptive, so willing to take in this generous gift of touch and connection she offered.

I continued to see them at many more events, including more Cuddle Parties, and eventually they got married: that evening of lowering defenses, of allowing another to generously give, gave them both a chance to dance in that harmonious flow of unconditional giving and receiving, which for them led to an outcome they had both longed for, but which was manifested only when they were ready to receive it, and each other, fully.

Throughout the past six years of my leading Cuddle Parties, many, many attendees have called upon my help. They have asked me their most shame-filled questions, whispered challenges or concerns that their interactions have brought up. They have sobbed in my arms – many of them crying in front of others for the first time ever. Each time, I feel so grateful to be the "life guard on duty," reminding everyone in the room that we are never truly alone: when we dare to bring our raw, gooey, vulnerable self and ask for help, we open ourselves to receive all the love, compassion, understanding, strength, joy, and acceptance that most people are longing to give. Most people are just waiting for an opening, an opportunity, to give.

"Even after all this time the sun never says to the earth, 'You owe me.' Look what happens with a love like that. It lights the whole sky." - Hāfiz

EXERCISES FOR RULE #8

1. Let's develop those receiving muscles. For the rest of this week, the invitation is for you to get as many compliments as possible. From yourself, your partner, your family, coworkers, or anyone else you can bring in. Your job is to "take it" – just breathe, after each compliment is given. Allow yourself to fully accept and receive it. In return, offer a simple, "Thank you"; you do not need to offer a compliment back. Take notes about how it feels, the thoughts you may have, the sensations in your body; notice what happens as the week goes on and you really get to practice the art of receiving.

2. It's time to shake up your "normal" routine. For the next 24 hours, if you are used to cooking and having your partner clean up, trade positions. If you are use to driving, ask a friend to drive, while you experience being driven. If you are the one who initiates touch, try saying you are open to touch, and then sit back and see who may come your way, and what touch may be offered. Try to dissect the ways in which you naturally give or you naturally receive, and see what happens when you consciously allow and invite the opposite. It's only for a day, so relax! Enjoy the "research and development" – take note of what arises, delights, or challenges. Most important, enjoy the ride!

Rule #9: Tears and Laughter (All Emotions) Are Welcome Here

"All that this world needs is a good cleansing of the heart of all the inhibitions of the past. And laughter and tears can do both. Tears will take out all the agony that is hidden inside you and laughter will take all that is preventing your ecstasy. Once you have learned the art you will be immensely surprised." ~ Osho

"When we want to run, we can choose to stay. When we wish to hide, we can choose not to. When we feel like closing up, we can choose to open up instead. It's always a choice. A choice between fear and love. When we choose fear, we persevere, when we choose love, we allow. Love's always allowing, inclusive and willing. Fear gives us a limited option, but love's always limitless." ~ Polona Somrak

"We're in a free fall into future. We don't know where we're going. Things are changing so fast, and always when you're going through a long tunnel, anxiety comes along. All you have to do to transform your hell into a paradise is to turn your fall into a voluntary act. It's a very

interesting shift of perspective and that's all it is ... joyful participation in the sorrows and everything changes." ~ Joseph Campbell

Rule Number Nine begins like this, "I declare this a safe space for tears as well as laughter. Some people have had a hard day, some people have had a hard week, and some people have had a hard life. Touch can be very healing, so new thoughts and feelings may arise. Sometimes just relaxing can allow the stresses of the week to fall out in the form of tears. It's fine. It's natural, and whatever, *whatever* comes up for you is welcomed here."

Cuddle Party is about setting the stage for people to have a safe space to give themselves permission to just feel. How often in life do we hold back? Afraid of the consequences if we show our anger to a boss, our tears to a parent or partner, our frustration or confusion to a beloved teacher, our joy to those who seem to be worse off than we are. What if we had a genuinely safe space to practice allowing all those cooped-up, repressed, held-back emotions a place to bubble up and be felt? That is one of the greatest gifts of Cuddle Party.

For me, there have been so many days or nights when I have locked myself in the bathroom to just sob - after a really touching movie, an encounter with someone who particularly strummed my heart strings, or the grief of my heart breaking, usually from a loss of connection - I have always felt sorrow or joy *so* deeply!! I spent the majority of my life trying to hide my raw vulnerability, especially my seemingly endless capacity for tears. My tears weren't honored as a child: the compassion and nurturing, that I sought, never came. Instead I was taught that to cry in front of another was to show them weakness. My vulnerability was used as a weapon against me, and my tears in public made others feel uncomfortable. That is what resulted in my sheltering in the bathroom, sobbing - often for hours on end - when the tears couldn't possibly be held back another minute. I would stay in there, in the dark, until the tears would stop falling and I could reset myself internally.

As an adult, I began trying again, opening myself up with my husband and children. But they didn't know what to do with my tears either, sure that it was their job to fix me, to make it all better. So, hearing the opening words, spoken at each Cuddle Party, first brought me suspicion, then curiousity, then hope, then experimentation, then anger and mourning for all the time and emotions I would never get back ... and finally to a determination and desire to show the world, especially those closest in my world, that they have a choice.

In every moment of our lives, we could chose to express or repress our genuine feelings that are longing to come through. If repression was chosen, the feelings would build up inside us, eventually coming out as rage or illness. If authentic, vulnerable expression - whether of anger, sadness, exuberance, whatever natural emotion allowed to flow through us - was chosen and felt fully, we found that on the other side of that feeling there would always be another emotion. The beauty of emotions expressed is that after you have burned through all the pent-up, repressed feelings, you get the opportunity to feel what you are feeling *in real time* - not colored by past filters or perceptions brought on by repressed emotions.

A few years after I began facilitating Cuddle Parties, I met Kai Karrel, and he introduced me to his greatest offering, the Goddess Puja - or, as he lovingly calls it, "The Art of Adoration." This ceremony is composed of three hours spent sitting equipped with a beautiful tray of implements, talismans, and gifts. Two participants are at each tray, one on either side. On one side of the tray, the people will practice unconditional receiving, and on the other side the participant practices unconditional giving. During the event, the recipients remain nested in their original places, and the givers progress from recipient to recipient.

At each station, the giver - guided by the spoken instructions of the facilitator - uses one of the consecrated items, prepared and waiting on the tray, as part of offering a sacred gift of devotion.

The givers honor many different aspects of the receivers whom they visit - using fire, incense, chocolate, rose petals and much more. My absolute favorite station, the one I believe Cuddle Party had prepared me to be able to allow, is the element of water. This beautiful giver, sitting across from you, begins tracing a single tear (a drop of water from a sacred bowl) from the corner of your eye to your chin, and then another droplet from your other eye to your chin. This is done six times, slowly, gently, adoringly, as this giver is instructed to give back the recipient's unshed tears, to offer to the recipient a safe space where their tears, and indeed all their emotions that were not honored before, have a chance to be returned - the receiver gets a beautiful opportunity for a reawakening, for having every last tear and repressed emotion lovingly held, without judgment or agenda, with no consequences, no payments due: just a few precious minutes that often seem like lifetimes as you reclaim all those magnificent feelings.

I have had the chance to have my tears and emotions held by Kai, and by many others, in this profound ceremony, and every time - as soon as that first drop of water begins to be traced on my face - my own floodgates open and I have the opportunity to sob, as another holds space for all those times of crying alone in the bathroom.

I began to welcome each and every one of my feelings; every tear, every laugh, and began to invite every one of my lovers, clients, workshop attendees, and my children to *feel* everything. I began teaching that tears are just "orgasms from our eyes" - another form of release. I can now love sitting with and experiencing my own depths, and anyone else's who is brave enough to crack open around me. It's *all* just energy wishing to be expressed fully.

I have also been blessed with the opportunity to be a Dakini (assistant) for many Goddess Pujas with Kai, and in that role I get to be a sacred observer as twenty-five to fifty women receive the gift of their tears' and emotions' being offered back to them. Never, for me, does it lose one iota of the magic. I am supremely touched and transformed after every single one. There is such a beautiful space, it's indescribable until you have had the opportunity to taste it, to glimpse it, to experience it for yourself.

Permission to feel - anything, everything - and have another or others not try to fix, change, or shift your emotions, or take them personally; just to offer instead an empty container, a blank canvas, a clear reflection, that in the end simply says, "I love you more, not less, for having had the courage to show all of you to me."

I had another breakthrough last year. It seemed as though the more happiness or joy I was willing to feel, the more profound the sorrow, anger, frustration, or disappointment that would follow.

I asked one of my dearest beloveds, Lawrence Lanoff, if after every great expansion he would then feel an equal or even greater contraction.

He laughed, and said no, that had not been his experience.

He then posed an important question to me – if we can use the word "important" to describe a question that has changed my life, and changed all I thought I knew about feelings: "Monique, what if the feeling you are identifying as 'contraction' is just you not being able or willing to slow down enough to feel every last sensation or feeling that is longing to be experienced in *this* moment?"

I sat with his inquiry for a few weeks, evaluating what truth it might have for me, curious as to what would happen if I did allow myself to slow down, to begin opening to the anger, sadness, or disappointment as just another feeling moving through – instead of resisting the negative feeling, or (as I often did) finding an activity to bring myself back to joy, delight, or happiness. At first it was difficult. When I felt what I had always labeled as bad, or when I felt contracted, I wanted to get as far away from those emotions as possible; it was through breath, and consciously reminding myself to slow down even more – to allow the feeling even more room to be felt – that, little by little, I stopped being afraid of, or needing to fix or change, my own feelings. I developed a wider range of being comfortable with feeling whatever may arise.

Now I have fun, constantly finding ways to slow down, and just experience, open to, *love* whatever happens to be arising within myself, or within whoever I happen to be with in that moment.

So now I cry often, even in public, grateful for each and every "heartbreak," because – on the other side – there is an even greater capacity to experience more of whatever emotion is authentic and true for me right now.

This ordinary moment is it. We don't need to seek the extraordinary because when we allow ourselves to be at home in the ordinary, it becomes extraordinary. This is it! Reminding us that we can find the magic, the sublime in this next breath, in this body. This is the only life that you are living. This moment, as you read these words - your life is completely unfolding. This body is Nirvana here and now. ~ Josh Baran

Another thing covered in this Cuddle Party rule is that it is the responsibility of the facilitator, not the other participants, to hold the space for emotions. So everyone in the Welcome Circle is encouraged to take the night off, especially if their default setting is "caretaker mode." If they ordinarily feel more comfortable giving than receiving, we invite them to practice just receiving, for this event. A further instruction is that if Person A is cuddling with, or having an interaction with, Person B who is having intense emotions coming up, Person A may always excuse themselves and summon the facilitator or assistant to come take their place. This leaves Person A free to go have their own experience, instead of having to feel responsible for another's emotions.

I have been able to experience the "aha" moment thousands of times, in the hundreds of Cuddle Parties I've been blessed to run. Someone is in the midst of "taking care" of someone else - whether it is their partner, a loved one, or just a random person they happened to be interacting with at this party - when all of a sudden it is as though time stops: I see them look up, often locking their eyes on me; they visibly take a deep breath and their face softens as they either raise their hand to signal they need help, or are brave enough to just call me over.

They often apologize to the person they are with, for the fact that they have just realized that they don't want to be there holding the space for this other's emotion, that they are going to change their mind and go do something else. I watch as they get up, the struggle often still going on within them, a struggle between relief at not having to be there any longer, and the anxiety about whether they are doing the "right" thing. Can it really be okay to not take care of someone else in need?

But it's enough - the seeds are planted, and they get to try something new. I am with the person who is having the strong emotions. By now they are often feeling like they did something wrong, or that they are too much. I get the pleasure of reassuring them that they are doing it exactly "right!" After all, they just gave another person the rare opportunity to practice taking care of themselves, and - especially if the person I am now holding is a partner or close person in that other person's life - I get to share with them how this goes back to Rules Four, Five, and Six: that in their beloved's exercising their right to change their mind, to say no (to this other) while saying yes (to themselves) now they can trust their loved one's yes so much more. This leaves them more free to feel sad, mad, or disappointed, because their beloved will either have the desire or bandwidth to hold space for whatever is coming up, or they will say, "No, thank you," and move on to something else: either way, this person now has all the room in the world to just keep feeling whatever happens to be arising in them.

At one Cuddle Party, there was a couple for whom the dynamic was that he was very used to taking care of her, physically and emotionally. The depth of his care was obvious. Halfway through the night, as she was crying in his arms, I saw the telltale sign; he lifted his head, scanning through the space, looking for me. I saw in his eyes that he was drowning – feeling that to be a good partner, he had to stay and help her, but that right then it was the place he least wanted to be. After a few minutes, he silently mouthed the word "Help," and I went over to them. I asked them both if it would be okay if I joined them. She looked embarrassed to have me witness her tears, but after his enthusiastic "yes" she said yes too.

I negotiated with them how they would like to add me, and we decided that we would sandwich her between us. Over the next half an hour, I asked questions and invited them to share what was going on, for each.

She was able to voice fear – fear of her partner's having his own experiences with others at the Cuddle Party, and also fear of making him resent her if she forced him to stay with her the whole time.

He voiced his love for his partner, and how much he enjoys spending time with her, and that his biggest wish was to be able to interact with more people, as he had been wanting for such a very long time – but never wanting to hurt her feelings. I asked her what she was most afraid of; her reply was that he would leave and never come back. So I asked if there was a way I could support her, in allowing him to explore in a way that could also feel safe to her.

We all decided that I would cuddle her and hold her tightly on the couch, so that she could watch the room and see where her partner was. He, in turn, would have a chance to navigate and explore, and to ask different people to interact – and, along with that, he would check in, via eye-contact, with his partner every little while: if she couldn't handle it, she would blink three times, signaling him to come back. He stayed for a few more minutes, obviously torn between excitement about what was being offered – the gift he had been longing for – and the feelings that had been so deeply ingrained within him: that he should be vigilant and dutiful; that he should stay, and be with his partner's deepest insecurities until they were gone.

Then, with a last kiss on her nose, he stood up and walked over to a group of three people, cuddling and massaging, and asked if he might join in. She and I walked over to the couch where she could watch the room, and she lay sobbing in my arms for a very long time, occasionally looking up towards him. His eyes would meet hers, and I imagine that each time their eyes met, it was all she could do to keep from giving the call-back signal. However, she refrained; she just allowed all her emotions to come out as tears in my lap.

Eventually, he moved on to other groups, finding ways he wanted to connect, always checking in with the beautiful soul on my lap. After about 30 minutes, she was able to sit up, and her tears began to dry. She began opening up to me about her past, her family history. She began to experience – perhaps for the first time – the beauty of emotions as they shift on their own, once they have had a chance to be felt fully. She had the chance to gain a new reference point in her body, to experience making it to the other side of a challenging emotion without having to have her partner there.

He also visibly began to relax, and to make his own bold requests. When I made the "ten minutes until closing circle" announcement, she thanked me, and asked if I would be willing to help her go to join her partner and another woman he was currently in deep conversation with. I asked her what she wanted, and she said she wasn't sure, but that she would like to find a way to join, even though it was still scary and uncomfortable for her. I asked her how it would be if they all had their backs to one another, a threesome pillar of support. She wouldn't have to face them, but they could all be connected. She liked the idea, but still wanted to know if I would be willing to break in and ask them for her. I was a yes, and as we approached, she had a few more tears come back – but she was steadily walking over.

When we reached them, I gently interrupted, and made the request for her. Both her partner and the other woman were really happy to try it. The relief and joy was so clearly evident on his face – the hope that he could be a good partner *and* live his own life.

They continued back-to-back, eventually all three of them holding hands; they all stayed connected even during the closing circle.

That is just one of so many different examples and lovely openings I have had the pleasure of witnessing, and being able to help facilitate and navigate.

"Our emotional symptoms are precious sources of life and individuality." ~ *Thomas Moore*

What if we could examine our emotions, according to their most basic nature?

Anne Kreamer writes, *„We do not get angry and then have our blood pressure rise - rather, our blood pressure rises in response to some stimulus, which causes our bodies to experience what we have learned to label ‚anger.‘ What we call emotion is simply how we mediate between environmental stimuli and subsequent behavior, and the labels by which we mentally index those stimuli and behaviors for future reference."*

Anne also surmises, that we have always relied upon signals from the emotional state of others in our vicinity to be alerted to danger, to be cautious when they are alert, to be content and bound communally when they are happy.

Read more about Anne's ideas at www.beyondcuddleparty.com.

I love that idea! That every single emotion is just the momentary appearance of a universal tool that helps us to navigate our environment, and that helps propel our evolution. What a novel concept - instead of our emotions‘ deterring us from the path, they are helping us to navigate it.

I teach a workshop, with another beloved, which is all about the gift we give each other in our ability to sit with our own and another's emotions. We show examples of being able to train our reptile brains - which are pre-programmed to react usually with „flight, fight, or freeze." We show that, with practice, we can create more and more „lag" time between the instant an event happens and the way we choose to respond to it.

Much of this training is about becoming more accepting of your own discomfort around intense feelings - your feelings, and those of others.

103

We most often react when we desperately want to be anywhere other than where we are feeling the discomfort of anger, grief ... the discomfort of *any* emotion that, to us, means that we did a bad job with those for whom we care the most deeply.

As you begin retraining yourself to just sit in the fire of the discomfort of whatever feelings or emotions are present, you remind yourself that it's not personal. Any time someone is offering a direct judgment about you, it really has nothing to do with you and everything to do with some general desire they are desperately seeking to experience - from you, for that moment.

If they say, „You are a cold bitch," they are looking for warmth. If they say, „You are a disgusting slob," they are looking for order. If you can remain calm inside, and maintain openness to allow whatever feelings the other is desperate to let out, there will come a turning point on its own - a turning point that arrives by having offered the emotions the room that was needed for them to be felt fully.

Unless the person feeling them emotionally clamps down on feeling them all the way through, there will be an eventual shift.

And each time someone experiences the profound beauty of an intense emotion's melting and another one's taking its place, it gives them a new experiential reference point within their body, building their awareness that they have the ability to take care of themselves, that they can feel things 100%, that they do not have to change, fix, or do anything to be better, and that - ultimately - neither can their partner, boss, parent, or friend.

Your relationship will begin to expand and rise in ways you cannot even imagine right now. As you each gain experience in observing one another and the event that's happening, then - in the extended lag time you have created for yourselves - you begin actively choosing how to respond, from love, compassion, and a willingness to hold yourself and the other exactly as you are showing up now.

There comes a trust - a self-trust, and a trust in your relationship - that it's safe to feel, to show up fully, that all of you will be honored. This takes practice, patience, and a willingness to let go of needing to be right. The rewards are so worth it!

Reid has a great analogy. Imagine you and the other person each are holding an electric fan. Each fan is blowing towards the other. Now, imagine that the other person is feeling a lot of emotion - is very triggered. The person decides that, in order to make the feelings better, they need to take it out on you. So imagine that all of that emotion is loaded into a big bucket of shit. According to the old way of doing things - after your partner throws their bucket on the fan, splattering you and the whole room with what was in it - *you* would then bring out your own bucket of shit, usually twice as big, and holler to them, „You call *that* a bucket of shit? I have been saving *this* one for three years!" and proceed to dump your bucket on your fan aimed in their direction.

Each of you would escalate, until the room is so dirty that neither of you can even remember how it started.

Reid's idea is that whoever is the least triggered should take a moment to collect their senses after the shit hits the fan, and then go and unplug the fan. Don't worry - he advises - about retaliating: just unplug the fans, and allow space for the more triggered person to be able to burn through whatever emotion began the whole confrontation.

There is beauty in the practice of respecting another person right where they are at. We don't need to approve of, or condone, the other's way of expressing their feelings, but we can make the conscious choice to offer them respect and acceptance, as their birthright of being human. It starts as an attitude inside us, and then can blossom into a choice or behavior.

William Ury offers, „Respect is essentially a yes to others - not to their demands, but rather to their basic humanity. In this sense, respect is indivisible. When we give respect to others, we are honoring the very same humanity that exists in us. When we acknowledge the dignity of others we acknowledging our own. We cannot truly respect others without respecting ourselves at the same time."

It's really important to note, here, that this does not include abuse of any kind: emotional, physical, or sexual. Cuddle Party is not about teaching you to be able to allow anyone in your life to use you as their punching bag, in any capacity. If abuse is occurring, please get out and ask for help: those emotions that keep coming up are telling you to get away.

With abuse not in the picture, feelings and emotions are beautiful tools to help you uncover treasures within you and all those you interact with. You uncover them by fully feeling, and unconditionally allowing another to fully feel, whatever happens to be arising. And ...

How do you know what you are supposed to be feeling? It's whatever you ARE feeling.

There is one more important item that Cuddle Party offers, in this rule: In regard to emotions, this is also where we get to talk about attraction, arousal, and liking people. The freedom and connection at a Cuddle Party may be a bit disorienting and, just as you might be surprised to find yourself crying or giggling, you might find yourself really attracted to someone. This is perfectly normal. Our agreements are:

You are allowed to like people at a Cuddle Party

You are allowed to be attracted to people at a Cuddle Party

You are even allowed to be aroused at a Cuddle Party

You are just not going to act on it

I have found that, for many people, this is their first opportunity to cuddle, touch, or be held in a non-sexual space. Their bodies have often been programmed to respond sexually when being that close to another human being. I love that Reid addressed this part, doing his best to help everyone feel like whatever may be happening - or not happening - for each of them was okay, was perfectly normal, and all of it was welcome. If someone does become aroused, they are invited to treat it like any other emotion, without having to act on it. It will usually quickly move through, giving place to yet another emotion to be experienced.

How often in life do we feel like we should act on another's desire? During Cuddle Parties there is often friendly banter, and even some G-rated flirting, as the attendees are given permission to like and/or be attracted to one another - but there is no agenda or goal to reach, since the beauty of the space is non-sexual interactions. So, I have been privileged to watch women who have been abused in the past, who are afraid to go anywhere near men, little by little, begin to open up to conversation, to holding hands, massage, and often even cuddling.

I've watched as these amazing men give them room to make requests, to change their minds, to get to say, „no" to anything, and often - after having a few of those experiences - they end up curled up tightly in a gentle man's arms, either crying and letting go of past traumas, or purring and giggling in joy because they have never experienced being touched or held just for touch's sake.

Another occurrence, that may be rare in our everyday lives, but that happens at nearly every Cuddle Party, is same-gender interactions: men cuddling or massaging other men, and women with other women. There is such safety established in the Welcome Circle, and the setting of the container with the Eleven Rules, that the attendees often are able to trust themselves and one another to try new things - to ask, to say no, to change their minds, to learn how to receive ... and especially to allow their emotions more room to come out and play, to be witnessed and felt fully, as they get to practice in a place where truly, truly, *truly* all of them is welcome here.

I want to end this chapter with a story, and with some song lyrics, that brought this point home to me.

I have been traveling so much, these past five years, rarely stopping for longer than a weekend. In 2014 I had the opportunity to be at a New Culture Summer Camp. It is a campground in the West Virginia mountains, by a beautiful creek, where people come together for ten days of intense community experience. At this gathering they practice, full out, what Rule Nine offers us at Cuddle Parties - feeling all our emotions, having the opportunity to practice being ourselves, playing by our own rules and values, and having the community around us accept us unconditionally, exactly as we are choosing to be.

It can be a little disorienting, and even though I had been practicing this concept in short bursts with lovers and events across the country, I was still wary. I still had so much body-memory of trying so hard to be accepted and always falling short. During those ten days of summer camp, with my two teenage sons and about seventy other amazing souls, I was blessed to experience transitioning from that place of „prove to me you aren't going to leave, prove that you can still love me even if..." to a place of inner peace and gratitude, of knowing that there truly were people who accepted me unconditionally, no matter how I chose to show up.

The breakthrough came when Sarah Taub - one of my dear friends, and one of the leaders of that Summer Camp - picked up her guitar and began to sing „All Is Welcome Here."

She got halfway through it and, all of a sudden, it hit me: I *was* welcome here, would always be welcome here.

I couldn't stop crying - letting go of forty years of trying to prove my right to exist, and now opening to how I had always been welcome here.

When Sarah finished the song, I asked if she could hold me, and she said yes - holding me, being the placeholder for the Universe, offering me the nurturing and acceptance I had sought for so long.

For one of those moments that changes everything, I am so grateful. Grateful to have had that experience, grateful to offer a mini-version of it in every Cuddle Party I am invited to facilitate, and grateful to offer it now to the hands, minds and hearts of all who read this book.

(A few lines from…) "All Is Welcome Here"

(The original version is by Miten & Deva Premal)

"Broken hearts and broken wings bring it all and everything
And bring the song you fear to sing all is welcome here

Even if you broke your vow a thousand times come anyhow
We're stepping into The Power Of Now and all is welcome here

I took a deep breath and I leapt and I awoke as if I'd never slept
Tears of gratitude I wept I was welcome here

So bring your laughter and bring your tears
Your busy lives and your careers and bring the pain you carried for years
All is welcome here"

EXERCISES FOR RULE #9

1. I call this the curiosity game: the next time an emotion arises, don't try to make sense of it, or understand why it is there. Instead try "not understanding it." Open your mind to the possibility that not only will you possibly never know why you are feeling what you are feeling, but think how freeing it would be to not know, to not have to explain it. Open to the feeling, just allow it to be felt and – if a judgment or understanding about that feeling comes up – thank it and let it go. Open up to, be curious about, the infinite possibilities of why this emotion is showing up now. From this place of not having to understand or label it, you are free to just feel it.

    The easiest way to do this is to set a timer for 5 to 10 minutes, and then to sit in a comfortable position, close your eyes, and simply observe whatever feeling happens to be arising – almost as if you are the Sun, watching clouds go by. If you get stuck on a thought or emotion, simply notice that you are caught up in it, thank it, and go back to witnessing. The more you practice this exercise, the more familiar you become with your mind's process around your feelings.

2. From the book Mind and Emotions by Matthew McKay ...

    "This exercise will help you gain familiarity with your emotional responses, and perhaps feel more comfortable with them. The exercise calls for listening to emotionally evocative songs. The first step is to identify six or eight songs that have an emotional impact on you. Think of music that really moves you and seems to open something emotional within you. Ideally, the various songs shouldn't trigger the same feeling. Some of them might evoke sadness, some might make you feel hopeful or excited, and some might even make you feel angry. Over the next week, play each of these songs at least once. As you listen to each song, turn your attention fully to whatever emotions you feel and try to keep them at the center of your awareness. Whether an emotion is painful or pleasant, look for words that really capture the essence of the feeling. Name the emotion, perhaps also describing some of the nuances or subtleties of the experience. Write down any thoughts, sensations, or action impulses that arose while you were listening." As you begin to notice thoughts, sensations, and ways you may be moved to action by particular emotions, you can begin crafting your response instead of falling into familiar reactions.

Rule #10: Respect people's privacy when sharing about Cuddle Parties (Confidentiality)

"Confidentiality is an ancient and well-warranted social value."
- Kay Redfield Jamison

"The Universe doesn't like secrets. It conspires to reveal the truth, to lead you to it." - Lisa Unger

"To be left alone is the most precious thing one can ask of the modern world." - Anthony Burgess

"The right to be let alone is indeed the beginning of all freedom."
- William O. Douglas

Rule Ten in Cuddle Party offers: "We love for you to share your cuddle experience with your friends and family. Please do!" I often add, "I would love it if there were billboards, and airplanes flying advertisements behind them about Cuddle Parties, and references to them in everyday conversations. But when sharing about Cuddle Party, please remember to speak of your own experience, and not someone else's. Many people have jobs or friends or families where they may not understand about coming to a Cuddle Party. Mister or Mrs. Executive corporate person may not want the world to know that they are a weekend cuddle monster. This means that we do not talk about who was here, by name or identifying feature - except you are free to mention me, since I'm completely out there. This includes that, if you see someone at another local community event, or out and about at a local establishment, like the grocery store, do not go over to them and say, 'How about that Cuddle Party last Friday night?' Don't do that! Let everyone here be the ones to out themselves, at whatever level they feel comfortable."

In this chapter I want to make a distinction between confidentiality, secrets, and privacy.

Let's start with some definitions:

Confidentiality: A mutually agreed-upon set of rules or promises, that limit access to, or places restrictions on, certain types of information.

Secret: Something that is kept, or meant to be kept, unknown or unseen by others.

Privacy: The state or condition of being free from being observed, or disturbed, by other people - or a state of freedom from intrusion.

Confidentiality is so important in a world where people are having a chance to explore new things. It is vital to have a space protected by a shared agreement, so that anything that is said or experienced will not be talked about to outsiders without explicit permission.

I was so excited, when I first discovered Cuddle Parties that I went to three in that first month. Within six weeks, I even invited Reid out for Utah's very first Cuddle Party. I printed fliers, invited all my family and friends - I even put lettering on the back of my car, advertising the upcoming event. One by one, my friends stopped calling, my church community backed away, and my family ended up disowning me for five years.

I couldn't understand it. I just wanted to share something that had brought so much opening and clarity into my life, but they just weren't ready to hear about it – some of them today still aren't ready to hear about it.

Since I do a lot of outreach and teaching in the realms of touch, intimacy, communication, sexuality, and the like, I imagine that it would be very difficult for me to ever again get a "normal" job. My explorations have been a process in which I finally had the chance to reclaim my voice, and commenced the bringing of all my inner parts to my outside, and although I wouldn't trade this for anything in the world, it was very painful to be shunned by almost everyone I had been deeply and lovingly connected to.

So I understand the need for confidentiality: it allows people to explore their own awakening at their own pace. After all, there is no guarantee that a person will decide to tell the world in general what they have been doing. It is their right to never tell; to instead just enjoy, if they prefer, an occasional weekend cuddle, and then to go back to their life as it has always been – warmed, now, by a private little gift that they have given themselves.

What is the difference between confidentiality and a secret? I would like to present the way Reid discerns this: he illustrates it by what he calls "a practice conversation."

The phrase came to him one day when he was on the phone with his mother, and the conversation was following the usual pattern: his mother was going on and on, complaining about something one of Reid's brothers was doing. In the middle of her rant, Reid had an intuition about what use all this might be to her - what she might be getting, from this extended conversation *to Reid* about what *someone else* was doing.

He immediately asked her the following question: "So, mom, you are having a practice conversation with me, right now - right? Are you practicing what you are going to say to [brother] so you can say it in the most effective way? I will give [brother] a call in a day or two and see how it went, okay?"

Reid had created a win-win for himself by *forcing the issue* in regard to what had been, up to then, an unspoken, un-negotiated secrecy about his mother's complaint-marathons. The win-win was as follows:

-- If his mother accepted Reid's right to notify his brother about the mother's complaints (and Reid had that right, because the secrecy had never been negotiated and owned, by the mother; it had been only taken for granted) the rant-marathons to Reid would most likely stop, because for her there would be no more use in trying to hone her verbiage - Reid's brother would now know, in advance, what she was going to talk about anyway.

-- And if Reid's mother would *not* accept Reid's abolishment of the un-negotiated secrecy, then too, undoubtedly, she would quit with the complaint marathons to Reid.

Reid's question was met first with silence, and then his mother said she had to go.

The next time she called and began the same type of conversation, Reid again asked if this was, for her, a practice conversation - and, again raised the issue of his checking with his brother. After this second round, she never brought that stuff up again.

Discernment between confidentiality and secrecy is one of the greatest tools to help you to filter what others share with you, so that you are not left with the burden of a lot of secrets, or constantly juggling the question of what is okay to share with whom.

Reid's idea about this is that if someone explicitly owns the request to you - the request for you to keep something secret that they need to tell you - you can hold that space for them *if you decide to* (after all, they have *asked* you, and part of the idea about asking is that the person being asked can say "no;" otherwise it would not be asking, it would instead be the issuance of an order.) If the person does not own the request to you - if they try to let it be unspoken, or taken for granted - Reid's belief is that holding the information they give you can too easily lead to gossip or drama - for example, along the lines of, "What? You knew about this already?"

Reid's recommendation is that in such cases, you should consider what you have been told as being in the nature of a "practice conversation," where the person, who is confiding to you, really *ought* to be talking to the person they are talking *about*. And Reid recommends that you deal with it by treating the information not as a secret but instead as a confidentiality, which includes that you will explicitly set a time limit on how long you will hold it.

To use Reid's practice conversation formula, you first need to set up a peer support group - or join one, if you know a group whose methods and philosophy are compatible. Three to five people is a good number, to cover the eventualities of busy schedules.

They must, of course, be individuals you can depend on to deal objectively with what you tell them. Here is a way of making that request that has worked for me: "Do you have the ability to treat what I am sharing with you as just a snapshot-moment in time, given from my point of view?" You do not need them to agree with things you may say, or to take your side on issues.

They must also be ready to do the work of holding you accountable. When you do have a practice conversation with someone in your peer group, your agreement with them is that they *will* check in, after a certain set time, with the person you were talking about. They will check in with that person, to make sure you have gone ahead and had the conversation you practiced.

So here is how it goes. I would say, "Reid, do you have time for a practice conversation?" If he says "yes," I proceed to share those things that I am wanting to tell someone else.

Reid would then offer back some useful information to help me better say what I want to say. He might point out changes or tweaks to my delivery, that might help that person be more able to hear me.

At the conclusion, Reid will say, "Okay, I will check in with so-and-so in seventy-two hours, and ask how the conversation went." I thus have three days to get my conversation done. Reid *will* call, after the seventy-two hours, and just say, "Hey, did Monique have a conversation with you this week about [the issue]?" If the person says "no," then Reid offers that they may want to call me for a conversation about it. With that, his responsibility in the matter ends.

Another super useful way to use a practice conversation is for working through things with someone with whom you are not currently in communication, whether because of distances, or personal decisions - it can even be someone who has died. A loved one, or someone from your peer group, can stand in for them. This can be a valuable tool for clearing out unsaid conversations that may be rattling around within you, taking up energy and bandwidth.

For example, I might ask Reid to stand in for my grandma (who passed away) and when we were ready, I might say, "Grandma, there is something I haven't been telling you," or "Grandma, there is something I have always wanted to say." Then I would share all the things I wish I could be sharing with my grandma, as if she was really there. Reid would just sit and receive and, in so doing, help me to move through any of the blocks that the unsaid communication could be creating in my body or in my life. It is such a precious tool - a beautiful gift we can offer one another.

One other thing I would like to touch on, in this section, is the importance of having good "rant buddies." Not everything *has* to be shared with everyone - sometimes it is kinder not to! But when someone is unable to hear you right now, or you truly just need to blow off some steam, then having a few deep friends who can hold space for a five to ten minute rant can be invaluable.

Again, you want to choose people who can hold objective space, who aren't going to feel a need to defend you, or to defend the other person or people. Having rant buddies in different areas of your social world can be a help, so the people you are ranting to are not even acquainted with the people you are ranting about, and thus they have nothing invested in the outcome.

If you are serving as someone's ranting buddy, it is important to limit it to a length of time that is comfortable for you. I recommend fifteen minutes at most. Even a two-minute rant can do wonders to clear blocked energy, and can help reset the person to be able to show up more objectively with whomever they feel challenged. I invite you to extend and honor confidentiality where it works for you, to develop a support system that includes practice conversations as well as rants, so that the things you *do* share become more clear and concise, and can be offered with much more freedom.

C. JoyBell C. wrote an excellent work regarding secrets I have picked the juiciest part to include here: (read more at www.beyondcuddleparty. com)

*It is far more profitable for a man to be able to remain innocent and have
love and be healthy and to be able to watch his loved ones in good health
and in good love, than for a man to uncover all the secrets of the universe!
A single love, a single faith, a single trust, and one hope - these are far, far
better things to aspire to have! And this - this is the biggest secret!" - C.
JoyBell C.*

So now ... secrets! How often have your ears perked up when
someone was willing to share their secret with you? We crave the feeling
of mattering to those we adore, and what better occasion than when they
trust you enough to share something that they "haven't ever been able to
tell another soul"?

I think it's beautiful when we can establish connections in which we
can share anything with each other, but the challenge is when someone
is asking you - or you take it upon yourself - to hold something in that
affects you on a personal level, or that hurts you too much to keep inside
yourself, or will impact others in a markedly negative way. Your mileage
may vary, but my personal certainty is that secrets always come out - that
sooner or later, all will be revealed. So my advice is to find ways to enable
yourself, and those in your life, to share sooner rather than later.

In 2012 - I had an experience, involving some other people that was
very painful. Had it been spoken about then, it would have blown over
quickly, and all parties could have worked through their reactions and
moved on. Instead, a lover at that time, implored me to keep it secret, just
until he could put some things in order. I feared the loss of connection
with him, and felt compassion for his predicament, so I foolishly said
"yes" - and from that moment on, it ate me up inside.

A few months later I was in the hospital with kidney stones and
a kidney infection. Being someone who is rarely sick, to me it was an
unmistakable sign that what I had agreed to was not healthy for me or
for anyone else involved.

I then tried to walk a tightrope of being able to share my experience,
without outing this other person. It just got worse, and this led to over
two years of deep pain and disconnect for all parties involved. What finally
resolved it all was writing it all down. He and I both did this - at first, just
for each other. Then together we put it online, and the situation finally
began to heal: there was closure, and possibilities for reconnection, where

117

there had been none when there was a secret to be kept.

Three years is a long time to have a deep agony, grief, and fear of "what's going to happen when it does come out," all chipping away at your core.

So, I speak from experience, as someone who is used to sharing everything, used to wearing my thoughts and feelings on my sleeve. Sometimes ... it happens to all of us ... a secret can be made to look like a good idea. What I would invite you to do is to sit with all of your fears of what will happen if you tell; then sit with all your grandest hopes of what could happen if you tell; and then, from your peer group that you have been establishing, get some help in how you can be supported in sharing.

Secrets isolate. They separate. They make you feel alone, like you are missing out on all the love and connection that is constantly around you. In a Dutch study done on adolescents, researchers found that keeping secrets contributed to all sorts of social challenges. All of the subjects who were keeping secrets displayed the same problems: low self-esteem, loneliness, feeling isolated, being more prone to sickness and depression. The opposite was also shown to be true: when the adolescent volunteers shared their secret, when they allowed others to help them, when they let go of carrying the burden or hiding something, many of the earlier symptoms lessened or were completely alleviated.

"I thought about how there are two types of secrets: the kind you WANT to keep in, and the kind you don't DARE to let out." - Ally Carter

This is not to say that one should never have secrets. A surprise party, your private thoughts, information that you hold about a few dear ones, okay - but when it begins adversely affecting you, eating away at your confidence, or if it would adversely affect others around you, take a good look at why you are carrying it. Try to evaluate the toll it is taking, and then imagine how you will feel when you share, when it is not resting squarely on your shoulders any longer.

Aidan Chambers offers this beautiful piece of wisdom, *Secrets. Funny how, when you're about to be given something precious, something you've wanted for a long time, you suddenly feel nervous in taking it. Everyone wants more than anything to be allowed into someone else's*

*most secret self. Everyone wants to allow someone into their most secret
self. Everyone feels so alone inside that their deepest wish is for someone
to know their secret being, because then they are alone no longer. Don't we
all long for this? Yet when it's offered it's frightening, because you might
not live up to the desires of the one who bestows the gift. And frightening
because you know that accepting such a gift means you'll want - perhaps
be expected - to offer a similar gift in return. Which means giving your
self away. And what's more frightening than that?*

Which is the perfect segue from secrets to privacy. Privacy is the right we
each have to our own internal and external space.

Each of us has different privacy settings. I have friends who live "off
the grid" - if solar energy can't provide it, they don't give a hoot about it;
who would never post anything on social media sites, who value having
the least amount of exposure of their personal lives.

I can appreciate their high regard for their own personal space. I,
Reid, and many other dear friends have a very different setting. We share
everything, and let others opt in or out according to how much they
want to know. For me it came down to one simple philosophy: if I am
willing to freely give everything away, there is nothing there for anyone
to take. That's what works for *me*. There is not a uniform, right-or-wrong
privacy level that works for everyone.

As you begin to explore the concept, and to exercise your right to
privacy, it is the beginning of your own personal awakening to solitude
- the beautiful gift of enjoying being alone with yourself. Albert Camus
said, *"In order to understand the world, one has to turn away from it on occasion."*
There is magic that happens when you begin to slow down, when you
stop pushing yourself to succeed, to be better. As you begin to go inwards,
looking at things that frighten you the most about yourself, you begin
craving more time with yourself. It becomes a lot less about anyone
outside of you. You begin breaking away from the need for validation
from others - and from distractions and addictions. You start shifting your
value from more to less. Instead of thinking you can please everyone or do
anything, you begin by pleasing yourself first, taking care of yourself first,
choosing what delights and excites you in each moment, and allowing
and inviting others along as their own path of delight and excitement
intersects with yours naturally, without effort or force.

For most of my life, the two conditions I have valued most have been connection and freedom. I have reached out, patiently waited for love, given and served - while at the same time finding my own self-expression, and trying to find the short cut, the magic answer, or the path to falling in love with myself.

I would catch glimpses of my own magnificence, but then my attention would slide off towards ways I could be better. I would beat myself up for not being able to stay in the "enlightened" states I sometimes reached, and ultimately would concoct another "crazy" Monique scheme in which I, and another beloved or several beloveds, would all win by teaching and traveling together.

I was always anticipating the next time I would see one of my eight lovers or various playmates. I love very deeply, but I was also adamant about not wanting a primary partner. I told everyone who would listen that I was my own primary, and that I did not not want to have to answer to anyone else.

Well … one day that all changed. I was on the road, touring, and I fell in love with someone, in a way I had never fallen in love before. I felt met in ways I had never been met before. I felt electricity sizzle through my entire body, heart, and soul whenever *he* would step into the room. I began experiencing, on a regular basis, connecting *while* freely being myself.

Those were some of the most wondrous and spectacular months of my life. But it eventually became obvious that although he loved me, he didn't feel the same as I did, and that he was not looking for a partner. Soon he was off on his next adventure, leaving a lot unresolved within me, and my heart broke into a gazillion pieces.

I had truly never felt such devastation. I felt utterly annihilated, and he wasn't available to hear any of it. So I took a few weeks, going inward, contemplating my options, and decided that instead of "moving on" - instead of looking for something to help me be happy again - I would instead take a long, honest look at where I was. I would invite and allow the heartbreak to override everything else.

I set aside my two biggest distractions, sex and sugar, and for the next two months had none of either. As of this writing I have been over 90 days without sugar, and I am hoping to go six months - to totally reset that part of my system. I am still not having "sex" but I have made love twice, after the two months of celibacy: instead of a distraction, both times were the most joyous celebration I have ever experienced.

During those two months, I had the opportunity to sit in one place for twenty-one days, the longest I had been anywhere in the last three years. I was at a retreat in the mountains of West Virginia. I facilitated a few classes for those who came to them but, for the most part, I was alone with my thoughts, feelings, stories - many that I had carried most of my life.

I got to sit by the slow-moving creek, surrounded by trees, and forest animals, Nature was the perfect backdrop for me to finally meet myself. I had been running and "doing" for so long, it was disorienting to just sit and see what came up when I was actually willing to put myself as my top priority. The heartbreak did not come from this other lover, he just illuminated how deeply I had broken my own heart, by abandoning myself for most of my life. There was a lot of unfelt anger, grief, frustration ... and under it all were two prevalent stories or scripts by which I had run my life. One: I had to prove my right to exist. Two: that by feeling joy, and by shining as bright as I can, my happiness and shininess takes away from others' right to misery.

I began to unravel all the validation I had sought from outside sources. I began to love my body, exactly as it was, instead of wishing for it to be different. I was even inspired to start the Facebook page, "Love the skin you are in" for people (mostly women) to be able to highlight all the parts of their bodies and themselves they have been ashamed of in the past. And towards the end of those twenty-one days, I found such a wealth of love from me to me, that I never again want to trade it for outside validation or activity. To me that is the ultimate gift you discover, as you explore what privacy means to you. You find the priceless treasure of solitude. And you know what? That lover who wasn't ready for a partner, when I "needed" him, has since rejoined me on the road, each of us meeting in the middle, inspiring one another, from a deep inner contentment.

My favorite author on this subject is Osho. Now that I have been able to taste this place he describes, it is as though he writes from the songs of my soul.

The passage begins with how absurd it is that people want others to enjoy their company, but that people don't really seem to enjoy their own company. How can you expect others to enjoy being around you if you don't enjoy being alone with yourself? He continues in depth explaining how aloneness, when one is ready for it, enhances joy which is our natural state. When we no longer depend on others for our joy there is so much more of it to find within ourselves. You become "enough unto yourself".

The moment you are no longer dependent on the other, language is meaningless, words are meaningless. In your silence – when there are no words, no language, nobody else is present – you are getting in tune with existence. This serenity, this silence, this aloneness will bring you immense rewards. It will allow you to grow to your full potential. For the first time you will be an individual, for the first time you will have the touch and the taste of freedom, and for the first time the immensity, the unboundedness of existence will be yours with all its blissfulness.

His wording is so masterful I cannot hope to do it credit, I can only share the gist. I highly suggest you seek them out at www.beyondcuddleparty.com.

I finally found my own gift of solitude, aloneness, and the spectrum of my particular flavor of privacy. While I enjoy sharing so much of my insides on the outside, there are a few sacred, deep parts that only a few powerful beloveds - or perhaps no one but me - will ever see. Not because of shame, but because of delight. They are so profound that there are no words that *could* ever describe what I am experiencing - and so it remains, rippling, expanding within the vast silence of my own being.

EXERCISES FOR RULE #10

1. Sit in a comfy place and give yourself five to ten minutes to do a combination of freestyle writing and meditative contemplation. Allowing yourself to imagine what the difference is between confidentiality, secrets, and privacy - to YOU. After you have thought about and written all three, take another five to ten minutes to brainstorm how each of them have served you, or not, in your life. Dare to be truthful, vulnerable, and raw with yourself. What is your current relationship with each of them? Finally, take five to ten minutes to imagine and write what your absolute ideal relationship would be to each one.

2. Now is your chance to "come clean" even if it is only to yourself. Think about three people in your life, from whom you have been withholding information. It could be a withheld compliment. It could be something you did or didn't do, that you have been too busy, angry, or whatever to tell them about. Write out the "secrets" you have been carrying, and - if you are a "yes" - go share it with the people whom it's about. If you can't yet bring yourself to do that, you can have your own releasing ritual. Build a fire, read what you have written, apologize in whatever manner helps you to release your own shame or guilt, and throw your paper into the fire. Watching as it burns, allow the flames to release you as you let go - and then reclaim all that space inside of you, that had been used to hold your secrets.

Rule #11: Keep the Cuddle Space Tidy

"The first step in the acquisition of wisdom is silence, the second listening, the third memory, the fourth practice, the fifth teaching others."
-Solomon Gabriol

"Revolution begins with one courageous soul, and can become a gorgeous contagion." – Eve Ensler

"You cannot be lonely if you like the person you're alone with."
— Wayne W. Dyer

Rule Eleven, the shortest rule of all states, "You are welcome to the snacks, and we ask that you keep them and all open drink containers out of the cuddle space. We have found that no one likes to cuddle in a puddle."

Sounds very simple and straightforward, but as with all the rules, there are multiple layers. Even though this rule is the simplest, this chapter has taken me the longest time to write.

You see, when my laptop, holding the latter half of this book, was stolen last November, this chapter was the one I missed the most. I had written my "perfect" ending before I had even started the rest of the book and, by the time I lost my laptop, this entire chapter was 90% completed.

Regenerating my book has been my greatest lesson in divine timing, and this chapter has brought the lesson home the most. I have known so much doubt - despair, even - as I labored to recreate this book while on the road. A lot of people were waiting on me, and I was feeling overwhelmed with an already super-hectic schedule that often included giving eight or nine classes a week.

But I managed to find pockets of time - days, sometimes a week or two - in which I could write and the inspiration would flow. Often what helped would be that I would read a book, attend a workshop, have a particular conversation, or experience a dream that would bring me back to a relevant memory.

Consistently, however, I found that each chapter could not have been written before it was. There would be key elements missing, that came to the forefront only a day or two before I was actually able to write about it. And this last chapter has taken the longest because whenever I would carve out time to recreate it, nothing would come out the way I wanted to get it across.

A few days ago, on August 30, 2015, one of my most cherished mentors passed away - one I met even before Reid Mihalko.

This was Wayne Dyer, the man whose name I heard for a great deal of my life, from my grandma. She had been the one person in my life I had been able to count on, my single stable point growing up, the only being who had offered me unconditional love.

Many times, when I would go to visit her, she would have the latest Public Broadcasting Service (PBS) special on, and would invite me to watch it with her. She was a big fan of Wayne, who - every six months - would present a new PBS special, as his contribution towards enticing viewers to donate during the semi-annual fundraising for PBS.

I admired Wayne too; what he was sharing went along with ideas and concepts I was beginning to develop. However, they remained ideas and concepts because I was always too busy with my sons, with my job, college, and reading or writing on my own to do anything further with them.

One of Grandma's fondest dreams was that she, I, my mom, and one of my sisters would all go see Wayne on one of his few Utah trips. One day she called me, and she was ultra-excited because she had finally done it - she had gotten tickets for the four of us to go see Wayne Dyer; the show would be in a few months. She was so excited, I couldn't help getting excited too. I was living in southern Utah at the time, and was a good four hours away from my beloved grandma, but we would talk on the phone most days, and every time before she hung up she would say, "X number of days until Wayne," and share another reason he had touched her so deeply.

About a month before we were all to meet Wayne, my grandma fell and broke her hip. She was placed in intensive care.

My oldest son Mikey and I jumped in the car and spent the next few days with her, trying to cheer her up, and enjoying being with her, and hatching schemes to get Mikey a ticket to come see Wayne with us - although by that time the appearance we were going to was sold out.

A few days later, after I had gone back home for work - assured by my grandma and her doctors that she was on the mend - we received the news that she had needed emergency surgery for a hole in her intestines. She made it through the surgery, but passed away a few hours later.

I was devastated - First because she, the brightest light I had ever known in my life, was gone.

Second, because I had not been there when she transitioned.

Third, because she never did get to meet Wayne.

After a week of heavy mourning, traveling for her funeral, singing for the first time since I was 12 years old (her favorite song, "Amazing Grace") I went to the public library and checked out all of the Wayne Dyer books they had.

I happen to be a fast reader, and I had devoured all those within a week. I then went to book stores and got the rest of what he had written. I began downloading online talks that he had recorded. By the day of his scheduled appearance, I felt I was as intimately connected to him as my grandma had been.

The event was bitter-sweet. Mikey now had Grandma's ticket, and we stood in line all day so we could be as close to the front as possible. We did get front-row seats - within our section of seating - and we were all feeling that my grandma was so close, as Wayne came out on stage.

He was as dynamic in person as I had come to find him in his books and recordings. He was a fabulous story-teller, sharing vulnerably from his own life to let us know that he had experienced everything he was sharing with us. During the break I purchased his three newest books, and he signed one of them for me. I had a moment to tell him that I was there because of my grandma - how she had not been able to make it, and how he had touched her life more than any other person.

He smiled and sent her his love and gratitude. Mikey grabbed a picture of Wayne and I together. Mikey later was randomly chosen to receive one of Wayne's books oriented towards teenagers - he was called up to the stage, and got to meet Wayne too. It was a truly incredible night, one that altered the course of my life.

The following is one of my favorite quotes from Wayne:

> *Passion is a feeling that tells you: this is the right thing to do.*
> *Nothing can stand in my way. It doesn't matter what anyone else says.*
> *This feeling is so good that it cannot be ignored. I'm going to follow my*
> *bliss and act upon this glorious sensation of joy.*

My life was altered in that, up to that point, I had followed all the rules - the things society says should make you happy and successful; and the things my church offered that were intended to make me worthy when I died and was able to go back to Heaven.

The only problem? I was completely miserable and had no idea who I was or what I believed in. Wayne was opening a way to finding my own passion, permission to go beyond the beliefs and limitations that had been set before me, and the ability to start making my own choices.

My favorite book of his, to this day, is *You See It When You Believe It*. I always grab copies when I find them in the used-book stores, so I can give them away on my travels when I feel called to. Like most people, I had spent my life waiting to see *before* I could believe. This is, now, hilarious to me in so many ways … I believed in fairies, God, Heaven, and Hell, but I did not believe in my own right to exist – I was waiting for someone else to prove to me that I was okay.

The series of personal events and losses that surrounded the night with Wayne, and the influence of that particular book, finally opened something inside me that launched my inquiry into myself. Wayne had believed in himself so greatly that, even as a child, he knew he would be on the Tonight Show. After he wrote his first book he quit his job and toured the United States, working as his own greatest cheerleader, never giving up on himself and his passion – and eventually, others began to see his brightness too. That was all beyond imagining to me, at the time, but within his stories there was a nugget of hope that perhaps somewhere I had my own brightness to share.

This led to my being brave enough to follow my heart to my very first Cuddle Party, only a month after having met Wayne. Which, as *this* book has described, changed my life in every way imaginable, and in some ways I never could have fathomed.

I bet you are saying to yourself, "What a touching story! And although we see how Wayne's encouragement is linked to Monique's following her passion, what in the world does it have to do with keeping the Cuddle Space tidy?"

"The most important journey you will take in your life will usually be the one of self transformation. Often, this is the scariest because it requires the greatest changes, in your life." - Shannon L. Alder

To me this rule always seemed to imply not only the literal cuddle space but also our own individual space. Being the last rule, it was meant to be carried with us as we would take what we had learned and practiced, within the safe container of Cuddle Party, out into our everyday lives.

To me, one of Reid's greatest sayings is, "Leave the campsite better than you found it." He uses it in reference to relationships with others, to leaving them better than you found them. But in all my studies, reading, and direct experience, the greatest relationship is within – so how do we go about "keeping our own inner cuddle space tidy" … i.e., leaving, on a continuous basis, our internal campsite better than we found it?

Don't try to change the world; just change yourself. Why? Because

the whole world is only relative to the eyes that are looking at it. Your world actually only exists for as long as you exist and with the death of you, includes the death of your world. Therefore, if there is no peace in your heart, you will find no peace in this world; ...
- C. JoyBell C.

(find the rest of C. JoyBell C.s insightful words on this topic at beyondcuddleparty.com)

I have met so many people on this journey, myself included, who want to change the world, to make a difference. But most of us begin in the wrong direction: we start by trying to affect those around us. We think the one who changes the most people is the one who makes the most difference. Guess what? The *only* person we are capable of changing is ourselves, that's it. The great irony is that once we begin being open to change within, everything without begins to change too - it has no choice: because you are different, so is everything and everyone else around you. We are each other's greatest reflections. Or as my beloved Kai Karrel would say, "We are each other's medicine."

Tom Althouse writes, "There is beauty all around us, and the light finds us when we realize we are all part of that beauty and worth the cherishing. If we despise any, we journey to despise ourselves. See all as beautiful, even if they choose to see themselves through you, as being less than so. We have the power to see for each, and be the reflection of what they may yet see."

I will forever be grateful to Reid Mihalko, Kai Karrel, Shawn Roop, Lawrence Lanoff, and Peter Petersen because each of them saw, recognized something in me, long before I could even imagine seeing it in myself. Eventually, as I took time to slow down, to redirect my focus inward instead of out to everyone else, I began to see myself. But it all started with being able to see and feel what each of these great men saw in me from the moment we met. They have given me so many truly magnificent gifts, but this - offering such a clear reflection of my brightest light, while still interacting with, loving, and accepting whichever Monique it was who happened to be showing up - is what helped me to finally start seeing myself.

To me that is key: so often in life, we see the grandest potential in people around us. That is beautiful, if you can manage to just hold a clear mirror, a vision of them in their grandest magnificence - because the more they hang out with you, the more opportunities they have to begin catching glimpses of themselves in that light. The problem comes when we start wanting them to change - or when we start putting yet someone else on a pedestal, start seeing only that someone else as divine or in their greatest potential: you begin to miss out on the lovely person who is right in front of you.

If you are even unconsciously waiting on them to change, it can be perceived by them as pressure, and instead of their benefiting from a beautiful mirror by which they could begin discovering themselves, they begin to resent you for trying to change them. Sometimes it can even make them feel worse about themselves, because they don't see how they can ever live up to what you are wanting from them.

One of the greatest gifts I have been given is that when I look at someone I see their soul: I get to feel how the universe loves them, uniquely. I get to fall in love with everyone I meet, because I'm introduced to their heart first. Every single person on this planet is amazing and extraordinary, but here is the thing: they are all of that, exactly as they are, and *you* are all of that exactly as you are.

We are each the gift, right now. The trick is to be willing to see the grandest expression - them, and you, whole and complete, while still interacting from a place of curiosity, wonder, and awe: allowing whatever parts of you, or another, are showing up right now, in this interaction. It is too easy to get caught in a space of dichotomies, too easy to want to hold on to things that feel "good" and to change the things that feel "bad."

> Martha Beck puts it so well: *We're used to living in an either-or world - but when it comes to yes-or-no dilemmas, what if both answers are true? What makes a yes-and mindset so powerful is it takes you beyond the two choices you thought you had. It opens up new, unseen possibilities. Try seeing your world and yourself this way, eyes open to what is before you, mind free of dichotomies. Are you good or bad, fragile or tough, wise or foolish? YES! And so am I.*

Another way to understand the importance of this rule is to remember how vital it is to keep our insides "tidy." Just as no one likes to "cuddle in a puddle," no one likes to wade through your internal crap, or to be held to the judgments you are still holding about yourself. We can be much better colleagues, coworkers, friends, and lovers to one another if we are consistently looking at and "cleaning up" our long-held belief systems, limitations, and the ongoing ways in which we are not accepting ourselves. One way of doing this is to develop a peer support-system, wherein you trust one another, and are open to honest feedback. You invite those closest to you to call you on your shit. You are open to having your own blind spots highlighted and pointed out, hopefully in the kindest way possible. It is not always easy to admit our own shortcomings, but nothing can be as valuable to your own internal growth. It takes a true friend to risk all that you have created together - to risk your anger, or your unwillingness to see their observation - and still be willing to point it out to you.

As you begin to make yourself your highest priority, other things that used to matter - that used to take up space, time, and effort - start becoming less and less important. It becomes easier to let everyone around you be exactly where they are at, to let them have the opinions and judgments they may have about you: it just doesn't matter, because you begin to see you. You begin to offer your own internal validation that you used to spend most of your life seeking from outside sources. Most of the people you used to chase after, and whom you most wanted to be noticed by, begin reaching out to *you*, because in your own inner peace, love, and self-acceptance you become a role model, a space for others to feel the same.

Cuddle Party, and its eleven Rules, was my entry into all of this, and eventually into myself. Perhaps this book will be your entry into you. Now that you have gotten to the end of the book, welcome to the beginning of you! This is not the end-all, be-all: it is a gateway, a beautiful doorway, beckoning you into the unknown, a launching point from which you can remember, and come back to, you. The world needs more of who you are! So practice, play, and remember; and know there is always more …

EXERCISE FOR RULE #11

There is only one exercise for this chapter. Take this book, and whatever has touched or opened inside you, and pay it forward: teach it to at least three more people, helping them come back home to them, and integrating what you have found, here, even more deeply within you. The best way to retain is to teach: go be more YOU in the world........

"GOD GRANT ME THE SERENITY TO ACCEPT THE PEOPLE I CANNOT CHANGE, THE COURAGE TO CHANGE THE ONE I CAN, AND THE WISDOM TO KNOW IT'S ME." – *Unknown*

Reviews

Destin Gerek

I have had the great pleasure of knowing Monique for the past five years, as both a colleague, as well as, a close friend. She is the representation of what I call "Powerful Vulnerability". It takes a very special power to be so incredibly vulnerable. To be able to share with the world your deepest wounds, perceived flaws, and life challenges. And being so vulnerable is itself such a powerful act with its impact on the person expressing it, as well as, on all those who are touched by it. Monique translates that powerful vulnerability through her new book "Cuddle Party" in a way that is guaranteed to both touch your heart and your life, as well as, inspire you to express more powerful vulnerability yourself.

"Cuddle Party" is more than just a detailed description of the rules of Cuddle Parties, it is a guidebook to living a more vulnerable, more powerful, more connected, more authentic life.

Arden Leigh

"If I could, I would send Monique Darling into your home. She would greet you with her wide smile that seems to radiate sunshine and the kind of hug that is simultaneously warm and nurturing while also making you feel in that moment like you're the only other person in the world, and then she would call you honey and sit down across from you, her body squared toward you and her face tranquil and calm letting you know that she is taking in every single word you say, and you would feel anything and everything you've been holding back suddenly come bubbling to the surface and immediately dissipating into the air between you, and you would both take a deep breath together and feel the miraculous capacity for healing that comes from the profound and yet stupidly simple act of being truly present with another person. But since I can't send Monique into your home, please read her book and experience her life changing story. It's the next best thing." - Arden Leigh, author of The New Rules of Attraction

Lawrence Lanoff

When you think of a person changing their entire life because of an experience - you have to think of Monique Darling. Monique's entire life changed when she discovered the power of cuddling. Cuddle party gave Monique a set of rules that she could begin creating an entirely different life out of.

Those rules became the basis of Monique's entire life. In this incredible book, she details each cuddle party rule - and the way that rule influenced and changed her life.

And it will do the same for you.

If there is ONE book to buy this year - it's Monique's book "Cuddle Party"

Lawrence Lanoff

Creator of The Art Of Radical Self Acceptance™ and The 5 Games of Life™

www.lawrencelanoff.com

Charlie Glickman

What would it be like if everyone in the world knew how to tune into their true desires, ask for what they want, accept or decline invitations without guilt, and honor boundaries and desire at the same time? It would be a pretty amazing thing, wouldn't it? Cuddle Parties are an incredible opportunity to learn how to create a little piece of that world in your own life. I've been to many of them and as a sex & relationship coach, I send a lot of my clients to them because I've seen how they facilitate powerful personal growth.

Monique Darling's book takes the wisdom and experience of a veteran Cuddle Party facilitator and distills it down into the core of the experience. Her compassion, care, and wisdom shine through her words, just as they do if you're lucky enough to meet her in person. And if you're curious (or nervous) about attending a Cuddle Party, you'll discover that it's not as scary or as silly as it might sound. Pick up a copy of this book, check it out, and maybe even sign up for a party sometime. You won't be disappointed.

—Charlie Glickman, sex & relationship coach

www.makesexeasy.com

Edie Weinstein

Can I possibly share more juicily and joyfully about this book, its author and the impact that it will have on the world? Not likely. Monique Darling has penned an essential book on relationships, communication, boundary setting....oh and cuddles, snuggles, spooning, nuzzling, massage and thousands of p.j.-clad people who have attended a workshop called Cuddle Party.

From the opening chapter that lays out the story of how her love affair with the community- building, body, mind and spirit healing event began to the final pages which honors one of her mentors (and mine), Wayne Dyer, the book is a cozy, warm and fuzzy frolic. You will want to dive into the 'puppy pile' and experience it vicariously through Monique's descriptions and then attend one yourself.

Cuddle Party has 11 rules that help create the safe container for the rest of the workshop to follow and each chapter of the book puts them into perspective. Through the lens of Monique's life experiences (and she is nakedly candid about them), the rules are a reflection of her healing. She observes that they come in handy for nearly every eventuality in our relationships with others as well as the woman or man in the mirror.

There are exercises you can put into practice immediately throughout the book that incorporate concepts that are central to Cuddle Party. As cosmic coincidence would have it, Monique was called on to walk the talk she espouses when her laptop computer containing many chapters of the book, was stolen and she had to recreate them while grieving their loss and the loss of the machine into which she had so lovingly placed them. She turned to the people in her life whom she most treasured and they held her through it as she baptized the book with her tears.

One of the things I treasure most about Monique and the book that is coming into the world, is their pure authenticity that are solid and grounded. As a Cuddle Party facilitator myself, I know how it has changed lives, opened hearts and improved relationships- mine included. I give *Cuddle Party: How Pajamas, Human Connection and 11 rules Can Change Your Life* a huge Hell Yes! (as Monique likes to say) and Monique the biggest hug-cuddle-nuzzle imaginable.

Edie Weinstein, LSW- Cuddle Party facilitator #27, journalist, transformational speaker, radio host, interfaith minister, social worker and author. **www.opti-mystical.com**

Shawn Roop

The word "rules" can invoke a concept of law for some. Monique's Darling's book is not a book of rules, it's more a book of observations, wisdom and guidelines on her journey through very rough and tumultuous landscape called life. The backdrop is of Cuddle Parties, relationships and dealing with one's own past. But the real treasure is in what is gained from the journey she takes us on with her, giving us permission to share these learned gifts with her. It's a perfect companion for anyone stepping out on their journey to self discovery.

Or in other words, "An epic tale of one woman's journey deep into the heart of intimacy to find the unmarked treasure. A story full of dangerous emotion traps, navigating complicated social experiments, love found, and lost, and the magnificent boundaries created to support experiences unimaginable. It's a heroic rise of one soul while practicing 11 Cuddle Party rules!" Who would read that?

Betty Martin

Monique has written a book that shares her personal journey about touch - and lets you benefit from her insights. And who would have thought that the Cuddle Party rules apply to life? Monique shows us exactly how. Thank you, Monique!

Alex S. Morgan

If you, your clients, or your family could use a reference guide to setting boundaries and deepening intimacy that supports your most authentic self, I highly recommend "Cuddle Party: How Pajamas, Human Connection, and 11 Rules Can Change Your Life." Monique Darling's eagerly-awaited book has a blend of inspiration, raw vulnerable truth, and guided exercises structured to help you explore the meaning of each rule in your life. As a relationship coach and sexuality educator, I'm always looking for resources to share that support my clients' journeys. This is a handbook written by someone who has been on that journey and, instead of showing you where she's been, challenges you to self-inquiry, supporting you on every page in seeking what she sought. This would be a great gift for teens and college students to help them develop a deeper understanding of consent and how to tune into their own wants and needs when they're juggling internal or external expectations. At the same time, there's something in this book to stretch you no matter how far along this path you are, if you're willing to push your edges. Go nab yours!

– Alex S. Morgan, relationship coach, sexuality educator, and editor of the forthcoming Guide to Inclusive Sex Education

References

www.cuddleparty.com – The official website of Cuddle Party. This is THE resource to find cuddle parties in your area, to find facilitators in your area, or even to find out how to become one.

www.reidaboutsex.com – Reid Mihalko. The founder of Cuddle Party, the man who wrote the rules. Now, as always; Reid's main goal is to get us to TALK. About sex, about fears, about feelings. To walk towards "the gun", to embrace our fears.

www.awakenbodyandsoul.com – Peter Petersen. Qi-gong instructor, Wellness Coach. If you are looking for inspiration on how to unstick all the stored up energy you have collected in your body, mind, heart, Peter is the best there is at helping you play fearlessly, move fluidly in every aspect of your life. He helps his clients become their own health advocate and regain a sense of stability, peace, and well-being into their everyday lives.

www.tantraquest.com – Shawn Roop. No labels. No definitions. No Jargon, or Code Words. But if you want to live a life well lived, Shawn has some keen ideas he'd love to share.

www.soullight.com – Lawrence Lanoff. Reality Hacker. If you are having trouble getting around belief systems that no longer serve you, I can think of no better referral to give you. If you let him, he will help you strip off all that you think, and step forth into what is.

www.kaikarrel.com – Kai Karrel. The Mystic. Years of fully immersing himself in religions as diverse as Christianity, Judaism, Hare Krishna, and others have resulted in a man truly capable of helping you find the diety within yourself, and worshipping it with sincere devotion.

www.makesexeasy.com – Charlie Glickman. The Wordsmith. Charlie can take the most controversial of topics, the most difficult things to discuss and talk about them in such a matter of fact effortless way, boil the topics down to their primary constituents. He just makes it so easy.

ardenleigh.typepad.com -- Arden Leigh. The Seductress. Seduction is the art of getting someone to do what they want to do. Just think of her has the ultimate advocate of self-permission. She is entheogen in human form. The more you get to know her the more your perceptions may change.

www.embodiedman.com – Destin Gerek. Erotic Rockstar. Get in tune with your inner archetypes. Your embodiment of success, your embodiment of sex, your embodiment of worship, and bring it to the surface. Become your own hero.

https://about.me/alexsmorgan -- Alex S. Morgan. If you are having trouble accepting your own identity, or being accepted; whether it is gender identity, or sexual identity, or sexual preferences, or even simply dealing with society's identity; Alex has a wealth of experience to offer you.

www.loveandsexmastery.com -- Seva Khalsa. His very name means service. I can think of no one as gentle, as experienced, as accepting as Seva. He really has seen it all, and tried most of it.

www.juicyenlightenment.com -- Monique Darling. If you don't know my by now… go back and reread the book. Or if you just want to know where I will be follow me at :

www.whereintheworldismoniquedarling.com

cuddlist

www.cuddlist.com -- A resource for individual cuddle sessions. It is co-founded by Madelon Guinazzo who is a Cuddle Party facilitator and trainer of facilitators. She uses the same principles and guidelines to train the individual practitioners (cuddlists) on the site. We recommend checking them out for conscious, clean, consensual cuddling!